KATE WEINDORFER

The Woman Behind
The Man And The Mountain

A Biography of
Kate Julia Weindorfer
wife of Cradle Mountain Pioneer
Gustav Weindorfer

By
Sally Schnackenberg

DEDICATION

For Robin Burtt
A true Teacher who gave a country kid
a love of learning and the confidence to achieve.

Copyright
Sally-Ann Schnackenberg BA (UTas) 1995

ISBN 0 949457 91 4

1st Printing 1995
2nd Printing 1998
3rd Printing 2002
4th Printing 2007

The third reprint of *Kate* was dedicated to the memory of the late Robin Hadrill, Kate's grand-nephew, who died on 3rd December 1996. Without his support and generosity this work would never have been produced.

Published by
REGAL PUBLICATIONS
24 Wellington Street, Launceston, Tasmania
Telephone (03) 6331 4222

ACKNOWLEDGMENTS

This book would never have eventuated without the enthusiastic support of individuals and organisations who helped me to thoroughly research Kate Julia Weindorfer.

Robin Hadrill, grandson of Kate's sister Blanche Priest, was a mine of information and encouragement. He gave me unlimited access to his collection of family documents and photographs which formed the foundation of my research. I would like to thank him and his wife Ruth most sincerely for their support which was both academic and personal. My thanks are also extended to Hugh Hadrill, Evelyn Graves and Diana Peltzer, grand nephews and grand niece of Kate and to Hugh and Evelyn's wives Marion and Anne, who offered support and information, including family anecdotes, when they became aware of my research. I appreciated their help, personal support and hospitality. A very special thank you to Phyllis Martin who knew Kate personally and shared her memories with me.

To my good friend Nick Collins I convey my heartfelt thanks for the many nights spent at his house, the meals he cooked and for his support and friendship when I was in Hobart researching this book.

Thanks are also be extended to Dr. Judi Walker and Dr. Tom Dunning, Lecturers in History at the University of Tasmania at Launceston, for their advice, comments and personal support and encouragement.

I would like to thank Sheila Houghton from the Field Naturalists Club of Victoria who retrieved information for me from the Minutes books and correspondence and membership files of the Club which became the basis for chapter 4.

Thanks are extended to Tom Mumbray from the Parks and Wildlife Service in Hobart for his continued support of this project.

I thank Greg Richardson, Devonport Barrister and Solicitor, and his Secretary Ann Henley, for interpreting the legal jargon in the Wills, Affidavits and other legal documents.

For access to photographs and postcards I thank Charles Smith, Dorothy Filgate, Robert Brookes, Mrs. Trebilco, Peter

Sims and John Clayton. I also thank Peter for his personal support of the project and his photographic expertise.

The following organisations and individuals have helped me in so many ways and I extend to each one my sincere appreciation for their help:

ABC Radio; The Advocate newspaper; Launceston Planetarium (Queen Victoria Museum and Art Gallery): Martin George; Weindorfer Memorial Committee: John Pickford, Alan Richmond, Anne Stocks, Vera Tregaskis, Jenny Pearce; Staff of the Tasmanian State Archives, Hobart; Staff of Crowther Library, Hobart; Staff of the Research Library, Northern Regional Library, Launceston; Staff of the Research Library, Burnie; Staff of the Mersey Regional Library, Devonport; Research Librarian, State Library of Victoria; Staff of the Local History Museum, Launceston; Fingal Historical Society: Roxie Cowie; Kentish Museum: Andrew Keddie; Ulverstone Historical Museum: Wendy Newton and Craig Broadfield; Australian Paper: John Hitchman and Alan Keeley. Special thanks to Darren Rist for the back cover photograph. Also many thanks to Jean Braid, Ron Bramich; Glenys Brown, David Duff, Dennis Maxwell, Stella Sharman, Nick Sherry and Janice Wright.

Finally to my husband Peter and my sons Michael and David the biggest thank you for their interest, patience, support and encouragement.

TABLE OF CONTENTS

LIST OF PLATES

FOREWORD

This book is about the life history of Kate Julia COWLE who was married to Gustav Weindorfer of Cradle Mountain.

The motivation for the work occurred when the author, Sally Schnackenberg, accidentally discovered Kate's lonely grave in the old Don Cemetery near Devonport. The curiosity as to why Kate's grave was some thirty-five miles from her husband's provided the necessary inspiration which later formed the basis for the author's History major gained at the University of Tasmania's Launceston campus in 1993.

The research carried out by Sally has revealed an untold part of the history of Cradle Mountain. "The Woman Behind the Man and the Mountain" is a most apt title. I am certain that those of that generation, if they were alive today, would confirm the accuracy of the research for this work. This is a book that had to be written in order to reveal a more complete history.

The author's intense enthusiasm and constant persistence generated a willingness from all requested to assist with the collection of various pieces of information. The descendants from the Hadrill and Graves families (Hugh and Robin, and Evelyn and Diana) were all happy to provide photos, diaries, letters, family anecdotes and articles of memorabilia to assist with the research. Although at first reticent, we found it a pleasure to assist Sally as she was not only enthusiastic to obtain and explore historical data, but also had a strong desire to understand the character of Kate.

It is an honour to have been asked to write this Foreword and to express on behalf of the descendants of Kate Weindorfer, our delight that Kate's achievements have now been properly recorded as a part of Tasmanian history.

Robin C Hadrill
April 1995

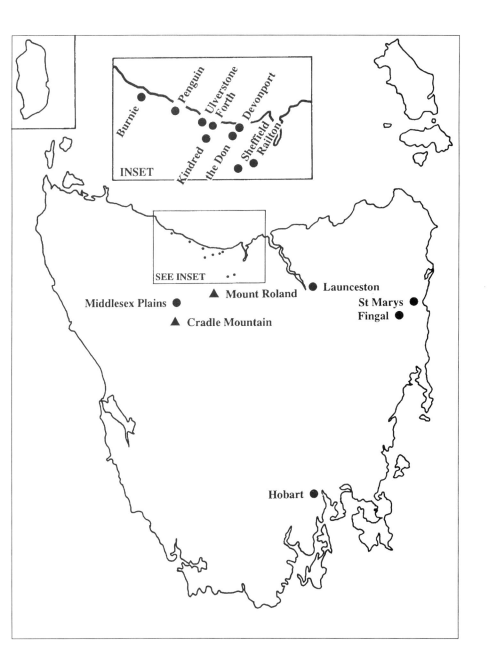

INSET

Burnie
Penguin
Ulverstone
Forth
Devonport
Kindred
the Don
Sheffield
Railton

SEE INSET

Middlesex Plains ●   ▲ Mount Roland   ● Launceston

▲ Cradle Mountain   St Marys ●
                                           Fingal ●

Hobart ●

INTRODUCTION

Visitors to Cradle Mountain come away familiar with the story of Gustav Weindorfer. He is often referred to as the 'hermit of Cradle Valley' and more recently as the father of conservation in Tasmania. Since his death in 1932 he has become a legend, depicted on the one hand as a hermit and on the other as a charming and congenial host to many visitors. Every New Year's day since his death, a well attended memorial service is held at his graveside near his home, Waldheim Chalet, at the mountain to honour his contribution to conservation in Tasmania. The placing of flowers and candles on graves at Christmas or New Year is an Austrian custom which was initiated in Weindorfer's case by his sister Rosa and continued after World War II by his niece, Rosita.

In keeping with this tradition fresh edelweiss is sent to Tasmania annually to be placed upon his grave. Those attending the service are addressed by people who remember him and afterwards slides and films are shown. A display of memorabilia in the chalet which now houses a museum enchants those attending the service. But in the annual eulogies to Weindorfer, Kate Julia Weindorfer is mentioned only in passing as having been his wife.

She is buried in a little cemetery at the Don, near Devonport. Since 1993 the Weindorfer Memorial Committee have placed flowers on her grave each New Year and in 1994 they attached a plaque informing the public that Weindorfer is interred at Cradle Mountain. There is no evidence on Weindorfer's grave that he was ever married. As Kate has been forgotten, each year the flowers are forgotten. Both times I removed the remains of them several months after the New Year.

The tragic irony of this is that if Gustav Weindorfer had not met Kate Julia Cowle at the Victorian Field Naturalists Club early this century and if they had not decided to marry, it is doubtful the Cradle Mountain legend would have been born. It is unlikely that Weindorfer would have come to Tasmania and may never have visited Cradle Valley; and the spectacular Cradle Mountain National Park, which was his vision, may never have eventuated.

Kate Weindorfer has been overlooked for far too long and one must ask why. Is it because the New Year remembrance day has created and kept alive a legend around her husband? Was her premature death the reason? Or is it simply because she was a woman who remained in the background behind a resourceful and charismatic man? This book will attempt to answer these questions, acquaint the reader with Kate, her relationship with Weindorfer and her role as a full partner in the Cradle Mountain venture and hopefully correct any previous misconceptions about her.

I have intentionally not researched the story of Kate Weindorfer from a feminist perspective. The method I have adopted is to concentrate on known information derived from primary sources where possible and then to present this information chronologically in chapters 1 - 4 with an analysis of why I believe she has been overlooked for so long in chapter 5. I have chosen this concept for two reasons. The first is that Kate played a real and important role in the Cradle Mountain venture and recognition of this fact is long overdue. The second reason is that I do not want her to be seen as an 'added woman' in an endeavour to comply with any real or imagined feminist conceptions.

The intuitive and impressionistic method of interpretation used by historiographers in order to gain maximum information from all available sources has been an invaluable tool. This technique has allowed me to speculate about periods of her life where information has been sketchy, such as her young adult years and the period spent in Victoria prior to her marriage. In these instances I have used the experiences of her sisters and brothers, which would have been similar to those of Kate, derived from family papers. This material includes personal letters from her mother and brothers to her sister Blanche and the diaries of her father Thomas Pressland Cowle II and her brother Dan which include direct references to Kate. Her sister Laura's expenses book has given me an insight into the day to day routine of the lives of the girls during their late teens and twenties revealing details of their clothing, hobbies and pastimes. Kate's descendants have told me anecdotes about her and Weindorfer which have been passed down orally through the family.

Kate was one of nine children born in 1863 at Fingal to well educated and astute pastoralist parents. Her mother ran a school for young ladies in Launceston prior to her marriage and her father made his fortune by farming and establishing a store on his farm at Branxholm to service the mining towns and miners on Tasmania's east coast during the mining boom of the mid 1800s. The family remained at Branxholm until 1879 when Kate was 16. Then she accompanied her parents and younger brother Bert to Launceston for a brief period whilst Mr. Cowle negotiated the purchase of a farm at Kindred on Tasmania's north west coast. Her family moved to Devonport early in the 1880s and her father became a prominent citizen of the town. The death of Mr. Cowle in 1894 when Kate was 31 and the settlement of his substantial Estate in 1901 when she was 38 was a watershed in her life. Her mother had predeceased him in 1890 and as a result Kate no longer had any responsibilities as an unmarried daughter. Her share of the Cowle Estate gave her financial and personal independence which allowed her to move to Melbourne with her sister Laura. She aimed to further her interest in botany by joining the Field Naturalists Club of Victoria in 1902. Kate was an active club member, displaying her botanic collections at meetings, contributing to the Club magazine and sharing leadership of field trips. Her knowledge of botany led to her friendship with Gustav Weindorfer, a fellow member, who encouraged and helped her to classify her plant collection. Other mutual interests, including music, strengthened their friendship and by 1905 they had decided to marry.

In chapter 1 Kate's family background is examined. Her fathers diaries have been the major source of information about this period of her life and I have been fortunate in that David Duff, a Devonport historian, has allowed me to use information from his unpublished notes about her father.

Chapter 2 examines Kate's sojourn in Victoria where she met Weindorfer. Details of her involvement with the Field Naturalists Club of Victoria have been extracted from the Club's Minutes and correspondence files for me by Club member

Sheila Houghton and extended using information from Dr. G.F.J. Bergman's publication, Gustav Weindorfer of Cradle Mountain. Dan Cowle's diary of 1905 detailed a visit by himself, his brother Charles and sister-in-law Isabel to Victoria for a fortnight to visit his sisters and to meet Weindorfer prior to Weindorfer and Kate's 1906 marriage. Dan's diary revealed the social aspect of Victorian life for Kate, her sister, fiancé and guests. The combination of these three sources has allowed me to reconstruct a reasonable picture of Kate's life during this period.

In chapters 3 and 4 the remaining ten years of Kate's life are explored and chapter 5 provides answers to questions raised earlier and is an analysis of what I believe are the reasons why she has faded into the background of Cradle Mountain history. The abundance of primary source material available, including her personal correspondence to her husband, has allowed me to gain a thorough knowledge of the last ten years of Kate's life. Her private roles of wife, sister, aunt, friend and employer have been given life through photographs, letters, diaries and other family papers which have been made available to me through the generosity of her descendants. Wills and other legal documents were accessed through the Probate Registry in Hobart. The State Archives house correspondence written and received by Kate, Weindorfer's personal diaries and letters and the diaries and letters of their close friends, Ronald and Kathie Smith. Past editions of local newspapers are available on microfiche at the regional libraries and it was from this source that I was able to read letters written to the Advocate and the North West Post by the Weindorfers about their Mount Roland honeymoon. The pièce de resistance of my research was the honour of meeting Mrs. Phyllis Martin of Devonport, who was Kate's maid from 1912-14. At the time of writing Mrs. Martin is ninety three years old and is the only person I met during months of research who knew Kate personally.

Overcoming opposition from her family, Kate married Weindorfer in 1906 at the home of her brother at Stowport, near Burnie on Tasmania's north west coast. After their marriage Kate's healthy financial situation allowed her to purchase 100 acres of Lauriston, Dan Cowle's farm at Kindred. The income the farm generated later gave them the means to purchase land at Cradle Valley and to build Waldheim. More importantly, it gave them the freedom to establish Weindorfers vision - a National Park for all people for all time. The Park eventually became self supporting as visitors happily paid for an unforgettable wilderness experience.

The Kindred property was named Roland Lea and was successfully established as a dairy and cropping farm. However, any plans they may have had of a bucolic rural life together were not to be because it was from the summit of Mount Roland, where they spent a five week honeymoon collecting and classifying plant species, that Weindorfer first saw Cradle Mountain. Its pristine forests and mountains were reminiscent of his homeland. It was to hold him in its spell for the rest of his life.

In 1910 they each purchased 200 acres of land at Cradle Mountain and their friend and neighbour Ronald Smith and members of his family also purchased 200 acre allotments, all on adjoining boundaries. The idea was to preserve as much forest as possible from logging. It was on Kate's acreage that the chalet, Waldheim, meaning home in the forest, was built in 1912. They spent many happy times there, initially in a tents and huts, then in the chalet, developing their tourism venture. At the same time Weindorfer trapped native animals for fur and meat and kept meteorological records for the Bureau of Meteorology in Hobart.

In 1914 Kate's health forced the couple apart for long periods of time and she was unable to join Weindorfer at the mountain as much as before. Various doctors diagnosed her condition as heart disease, lung complaints and indigestion, and according to her death certificate she died as the result of a debilitating kidney disease. However, in a letter to Weindorfer in 1915 she wrote of a lump in her left breast which caused her doctor to send her to Launceston to be x-rayed. The lump should not be overlooked amongst the conflicting diagnoses because her painful and drawn out death may have been the result of breast cancer. The true cause of her death will remain unknown. She died on 29 April 1916, three months before her 53rd birthday.

Her brief ten year marriage to Weindorfer afforded her great happiness and contentment. She loved him unconditionally and missed him very much during his long absences at the mountain. She spent many hours writing letters to him and reading and rereading his replies. Phyllis Martin (nee Granger), who was only twelve years old when she began to work for Kate in 1914, was a great comfort to her. Phyllis and Kate were very fond of one another and she has many warm memories of her. Phyllis describes Kate as having been 'a lovely, kind and gentle woman with long dark hair. I liked her very much.' However, she adds, 'she was left on her own far too much.'[1] After Kate's death Weindorfer moved permanently to the mountain to live and continued their tourism enterprise and his push to have the area officially declared a National Park until his own death sixteen years later. He did not remarry.

'The man and the mountain': how smoothly the words roll from the tongue. The popular legend of Gustav Weindorfer, the lone man battling the elements and taming the wilderness is not entirely true. It is true that he created the concept of wilderness holidays in Tasmania and spent a great deal of time alone at the mountain, especially after Kate's death. But he was not a loner by choice. He enjoyed the company of other people and after Kate died his move to the mountain was not a freely made choice. It occurred largely as a result of anti-German hostility directed at him by the people from the Devonport/Ulverstone area. Rumours were spread that he was a German spy, his dog was poisoned and he was asked to sever his connection with the Ulverstone Club. Some members of Kate's family blamed him for her death and also held an anti-German bias towards him. They made it difficult for the farm to be sold and for him to receive the proceeds as Kate had directed in a Codicil attached to her Will. In fact the farm was not sold until 1926, ten years after her death.

The Gustav Weindorfer legend has been reiterated by writers for years and it is reinforced annually at the Weindorfer Memorial Service. The final sixteen years of his life were solitary, but a solitude broken regularly by visits from friends and tourists. But for the first ten years of the Cradle Mountain endeavour, the most difficult years when the venture was literally carved from the wilderness, he was not alone. He was loved, supported, and joined regularly by his wife, his equal partner in the venture. She was the woman whose photograph he kept by his bedside and whose letters he kept until the day he died. The woman he called '... my best friend.'[2]

Plate 1: Kate Weindorfer's grave at the Don, near Devonport.
Photograph: Peter Schnackenberg

CHAPTER 1
Family Background

Kate Julia Cowle was born in her parents home at "Cullens-wood", the estate of the Legge family at Fingal on the East Coast of Tasmania on the 19th July 1863. Her mother, Emma Cleaver, was a retired school teacher and her father, Thomas Pressland Cowle II, was an ironmonger by trade,[3] and was employed as a store keeper in Fingal as a young man.[4] He was later given a land grant at Fingal and became a successful pastoralist and shrewd investor. During the east coast mining boom of the 1860s he established a store on his second farm at Branxholm, providing a much needed service for the miners, which included deliveries of food grown on his farm and other goods purchased at Hobart into the mining towns.[5] In 1879, when Kate was 16, the family moved to St. Leonards in Launceston for a brief period and in 1880 moved to Devonport where they settled permanently.

The Arrival of the Cowle Family to Van Diemen's Land and the Establishment of the Hobart Town Commercial and French Academy.

Kate's grandparents, Thomas Pressland Cowle I and his wife Mary arrived in Van Diemen's Land from England with their three eldest children, Anne, Emily and Thomas, who was only nine months old,[6] aboard the barque Auriga on 16 October 1833.[7] Mr. and Mrs. Cowle had lived in London where Mr. Cowle worked as an insurance clerk with W. Griffiths Ship and Insurance Brokers of Lombard Street.[8] Mr. Cowle had received a classical education and spoke several languages[9] which enabled him to move successfully into the field of teaching after finding it difficult to obtain suitable employment.[10] This was a career change which served him well during his time in the colony. Shortly after the family arrived in Hobart Town, Mr. Cowle purchased the Hobart Town Commercial Academy from Mr. James Thompson,[11] which was situated in a small house in Davy Street.[12] An advertisement in the Hobart Town Courier on the 27th December 1833 announced the opening of his school the following January:[13]

COMMERCIAL ACADEMY

Mr. Cowle respectfully informs his friends and the public, that his Academy for a limited number of Young Gentlemen as boarders, and Day Pupils, in the various branches of useful and commercial education, will open on Monday the 20th January next, at his residence in Davey-street, [sic] lately in the occupation of Mrs. Wells, where prospectuses and terms may be had.

The boys' studies included Virgil and Cornelius and their uniform was a cloth jacket, a shirt with a white frill at the neck and trousers with lots of buttons.[14] A broad brimmed leghorn hat completed the ensemble. Graduates from the school included many prominent doctors, lawyers and justices of Hobart Town and the success of the school was such that Mr. Cowle purchased a larger house at 13 Melville Street,[15] now owned by the Real Estate Institute, which he named Pressland House. The new premises, later renamed The Hobart Town Commercial and French Academy, boasted the addition of a large and well ventilated school room for the comfort of the boys[16] and a big secluded playing area, which included a tennis court,[17] ensured that they received plenty of fresh air. The house, which incorporated the family home, was elegantly furnished and two brick terrace cottages were built next door[18] and were named Norfolk Terrace.[19]

Plate 2:
Thomas Pressland Cowle I.
Photo: Courtesy R. Hadrill

Plate 3:
Mary Cowle, Wife of TP Cowle
I. Photo: Courtesy R. Hadrill

Plate 4: Pressland House, 13 Melville Street Hobart. Photo: Courtesy R. Hadrill

In November, 1846 the Hobart Town newspaper, the Courier, carried the report that because business matters might require Mr. Cowle and his family's absence from the colony for an unstated time, the school would be administered by Mr. L. Langley, a capable and well qualified scholar.[20] Langley was a convict transported for fifteen years to Van Diemen's Land in 1839 and given a ticket of leave in 1845 for good behaviour.[21] The Cowle's departed for England on the ship the Jane Frances on 21 January 1847.[22]

Kate's father, Thomas Pressland Cowle II was then 14 years old. He had commenced his education at his father's school[23] and completed it in England where he was afterwards apprenticed to an Ironmonger in Birmingham, but by the age of nineteen he decided to return to Australia.[24] He left his parents' home in London on 11 September 1852 and arrived at Williamstown in Victoria in January 1853 with £90 in goods and £10 in his pocket.[25] He was followed by the rest of his family who returned to Hobart Town on 26 November aboard the ship Derwentwater.[26] Thomas worked for a brief period in a store in Melbourne, then searched unsuccessfully for gold at Creswick and Ballarat before returning to Van Diemen's Land to rejoin his family[27] and to work as a store manager for Messrs. Valentine and Company in Hobart.

3

Plate 5: Kate's parents, Thomas and Emma Cowle.
This may be their wedding photograph. Photo: Courtesy R. Hadrill.

Establishing the second and third generations of the Cowle Family.

Thomas was sent to the east coast of Tasmania in the early 1850s to manage the Fingal store owned by Valentine and Company. He married Miss Emma Cleaver, in the home of her father, a Launceston ironmonger, on the 13th May 1855[28] and the couple settled down in a cottage on the Cullenswood estate owned by the Legge family at Fingal[29] in order to learn the intricacies of farming.[30] Thomas and Emma were kept busy farming and raising their growing family. Six of their nine children, Thomas, Freddy, Carrie, Kate, Blanche and Dan, were born at Cullenswood during the years 1858 to 1868.[31]

Plate 6: Kate's brother Thomas.
Photo: Courtesy R. Hadrill

Plate 8: Kate, aged about 8 years.
Photo: Courtesy R. Hadrill

Plate 7: Kate's brother Dan.
Photo: Courtesy E. Graves

Thomas purchased his own farm, "Wigton"[32], named after Wigton Hall, the property of his maternal grandparents in Devon, England[33], in the Parish of Haslemere in Fingal in 1869. He moved the family in on 15 April two months prior to Kate's 6th birthday. He grew crops and kept cattle, pigs and sheep.[34] Cheese was a major product from the farm and was sold in Hobart, Launceston and locally along with other produce.[35] He worked the farm with the help his eldest son Thomas, called Press by the family, and employed casual workers during planting and harvesting.[36] His second son, Fred, worked on the Cullenswood Estate nearby. In 1874 Thomas bought a new property at Branxholm. He let Wigton to tenant farmers and in 1875, much to the anguish of Emma, sold the property for £1,000 cash.[37] In the same year he was appointed a Justice of the Peace at Branxholm and manager of the local post office.[38] His three youngest children, Laura, Charles, and Bert, were born there.[39]

Plate 9: Kate's sister Blanche, held by her mother, Emma. Photo: Courtesy R. Hadrill.

Plate 10: Kate, held by her father, Thomas. Photo: Courtesy R. Hadrill

The mining boom on the east coast at this time brought out the entrepreneur in Thomas. It gave him the incentive to set up a store on his farm to supply the miners with fruit, vegetables, meat and dairy products produced on the farm as well as staple items such as flour, cloth and other commodities not produced on the farm.[40] On his trips into Launceston and Hobart he purchased watches, boots, drapery and jewellery for resale to the miners.[41] Accompanied by Press and Fred, Thomas delivered supplies directly to the mine workings and camps, one of which was the prosperous Brothers' Home tin mine owned by the Krushka Brothers,[42] and brought out packs of tin

6

which he transported to Bridport to be shipped out of the State.[43] For this service Thomas charged £3/10/6 per ton of tin.[44] He was so busy providing these services that during 1876 he was unable to find the time to write up his diary for six months, a task he usually performed faithfully daily. In 1877 Thomas bought a tin mine in Branxholm. However, he did not work it himself, preferring to rent it out.[45] No doubt his decision not to become a miner was influenced by his experiences in Victoria where he would have seen fortunes made and lost whereas merchants always had a guaranteed income.

The children were encouraged to be practical. They kept chickens and had their own little gardens in which they grew daisies, pansies, tulips, daffodils and similar plants.[46] When not at school in Hobart, Kate and her sisters helped with light chores, they milked the house cow and made the butter, jams and jellies, and thoroughly spoilt the family cat, Brownie, by giving him too many "tit bits" of liver.[47] However, their lives were not always work. They had plenty of time to play in the garden when the weather was fine, or in the barn on wet days.[48] Thomas named the dairy cows Kate, Caroline, Emma and Laura after the girls and their mother and Kate was unfortunate enough to be kicked by one when she was 8.[49] All of the children were capable horse riders and regularly accompanied their father on trips into Scottsdale and Fingal.[50] Kate was able to ride well from an early age and when she was 14 rode with her father from Branxholm to St. Leonards, which took them two days.[51] She was a proficient musician which pleased her father,[52] and played the violin, piano and flute. Thomas was a religious man and read to the children from the Bible and from the classics every Sunday evening without fail.[53] When a new public house opened at Derby in 1877 he lamented in his diary about the "sad work" it was doing amongst the miners.[54]

Kate left the family in April 1872, at the age of nine, to begin her education in Hobart.[55] Along with her sisters Carrie and Blanche, she was cared for at the home of her paternal grandparents by her Aunt Annie whom Thomas paid £12/- per year for the care of Kate and Blanche.[56] Thomas regularly corresponded with Annie about the welfare of the children and his parents[57] and he visited the children often and took them to the theatre and for walks.[58] Press and Fred would occasionally accompany their father on these trips and Thomas noted in his 1873 diary that the children were always happy to be together again.[59] There is no evidence that Emma accompanied Thomas on any of the trips to Hobart, probably because she had her hands full with the younger children. On the 5th September 1877 she miscarried her tenth child and was sad and frail for weeks afterwards.[60]

Plate 11. Kate's Aunt, Anne Cowle. Photo: Courtesy R. Hadrill.

The wet weather of the East Coast, which Thomas saw as being the cause for the health problems of several of his children, caused him to decide to remove the family permanently.[61] In February 1879, accompanied by Emma, Kate and Bertie he moved into Launceston where they lived in a boarding house before leasing a large house, Maplestead, at St. Leonards for six months.[62] He based himself here in order to inspect properties in the Deloraine, Latrobe and Leven districts.[63] Kate was a dutiful companion to Emma who fretted for her children who had remained at Branxholm. However she need not have worried because a visit home by Thomas in March found all to be in order[64] with Press and Freddy capably managing the estate whilst Carrie and Blanche took care of the household and the younger children, Dan, Laura and Charley.[65]

8

Plate 12: Kate's sister Carrie.
Photo: Courtesy R. Hadrill.

Plate 13: Kate's brother, Bert.
Photo: Courtesy R. Hadrill.

Kate helped her mother care for Bert, whose delicate health Emma was quite convinced was caused by the condition of the Launceston drains.[66] In a letter to Blanche, dated 8th May 1879, Emma wrote of how she and Kate decided to discontinue Bert's medications and gave him brandy and beaten egg, boiled milk and a little magnesia instead, which she said did him far more good than anything else had![67] In the same letter she wrote that Thomas had left for the north west coast to view the new farm he had purchased at Kindred, where he was very impressed with the land.[68] Thomas bought 283 acres of land at Kindred in April 1879 for £3/5/- per acre.[69] The rich volcanic soil of the region is ideal for farming and no doubt this lay behind Thomas' decision to purchase the property. On the 29th of May Emma and Kate visited the property, named Lauriston, and returned to Launceston to arrange for the family's goods and chattels to be transported to the north west coast.[70] However, Thomas had problems getting possession of the property and they did not move until the following year.[71] In the meantime arrangements were made to sell Branxholm and move the remaining children into Launceston.[72] When they arrived in June 1879, dancing lessons were arranged for the girls and Kate and Carrie attended garden parties and were invited to play croquet.[73]

Plate 14: Lauriston, the Cowle Family homestead at Kindred: built in 1881. Photo: Courtesy R. Hadrill.

Plate 15: Harvest time. Kate (in foreground with rake) and her sisters and brothers at Lauriston. Photo: Courtesy R. Hadrill

10

Establishment of the Family in Devonport

The Cowle's established themselves on the north west coast in 1880 but the Branxholm property remained unsold. The two elder boys remained at Branxholm and continued to manage affairs there.[74] Kate and her sisters missed their brothers and the Branxholm estate[75] and spent their days at Lauriston painting, playing contemporary musical arrangements on the new piano,[76] and tending the kitchen garden and chickens. They did the family mending, embroidered and sewed gifts for each other, trimmed their hats and occasionally made frocks.[77] Much time was spent writing letters to their brothers and reading their replies which included accounts of a gold rush at Mt. Horror and the effect it had on the local people.[78] The girls would no doubt have been amused by their brother Press's account of the innovative food preparation techniques he and Freddy were using:

'You say that you do not know how we make maizena pudding with out [sic] milk, we mixed it up with water, just maizena and water we have no nutmeg grater, but we use a horse rasp instead, which answers the same purpose.'[79]

The arrival of "The Great Southern Comet" in the southern skies in February 1880[80] was a cause of great interest to Fred Cowle, and he asked his sisters:

Have you seen the Comet? I have, on two nights, but it is rather dim owing to it setting where the sun does, soon after dark.[81]

Thomas purchased a large block of land in Formby bound by Little Fenton, Steele, Rooke and Stewart Streets and the family's town house, Alta Vista, was built there. This was a wise investment as a considerable portion of this land was later developed as the central business district of Devonport and its real estate value increased accordingly. The house was large and a stable and coach house were erected and substantial vegetable, fruit and flower gardens with rosemary borders were planted.[82] A lawn tennis court within the grounds was enjoyed by the family and their friends. The family divided their time between the farm which was managed by the boys, and town where Thomas played a prominent role in various organisations and boards. Their means of transport between the two homes was either by horse and buggy or the excursion train.[83]

Plate 16: Kate's mother,
Emma Cowle.
Photo: Courtesy R. Hadrill .

Plate 17: Kate's father,
Thomas Pressland Cowle II.
Photo: Courtesy R. Hadrill

The social lives of Kate and her brothers and sisters improved considerably by the building of the family's town house. Kate spent her spare time in town visiting or entertaining friends at home with her mother and sisters and some evenings were spent dancing at the town hall, Alta Vista or at the homes of friends. The women took advantage of the stores and local dressmakers to purchase dresses, nightwear, whalebone corsets, gloves and boots.[84] The family also enjoyed taking walks and attending local regattas, agricultural and flower shows, or horse races which were held locally or in Launceston and Hobart.[85] The younger members of the family spent their time rowing on the Mersey River, swimming at the baths at Torquay, or skating at the local rink. Kate's warm character and interest in conservation is revealed in entries in Dan Cowle's diary for July 1883: "The younger boys, Charles and Bert, had found an albatross at the float where the family kept their boat and Kate, who was in town, cared for it. She took it to the farm five days later and it was sent to Launceston via the morning train after a further week of nursing. The day following its despatch a letter was received from the museum regarding the bird[86] which had obviously survived."

The construction of two small public halls in Stewart Street in 1887 and 1889 by Thomas Cowle[87] provided a venue for wider entertainment including Grand Concerts, lectures, minstrel concerts, masonic meetings, dancing and church gatherings.[88] Kate and her brother Fred were very close, often travelling together between the farm and town.[89] Both were accomplished musicians and on 23 August 1888, they entertained about 250 people at Cowle's Hall, playing the organ and violin.[90] His suicide in November 1889, whilst the girls were at the Forth Flower Show, devastated Kate and the family.[91]

Plate 18: Kate, aged in her early 20s. Photo: Courtesy R. Hadrill.

Plate 19: Kate's brother, Frederick Cowle. Photo: Courtesy R. Hadrill.

Kate's mother died on 27 October 1890 and her father married Emily Johnson, a widow from East Devonport, in 1894. His death the same year from Bright's Disease resulted in Kate, who was then 31 years old, receiving an annuity of £50 which allowed her to live quite comfortably. Despite her financial independence, at some stage after her father's death Kate lived with her cousin, Florence Anderson, in Hobart. An accepted role of older single women early this century was that of the 'maiden aunt' who was always available to attend to the wants and needs of other family members. Her exact role at the Anderson's is unknown but she may have been a companion to Florence or governess to the two boys, Ted and Neville, the latter whom she described to her niece, Laura Hadrill, as 'a bad little boy.'[92] The Anderson's lived a life of comfort and elegance and entertained their friends in great style[93] which was enjoyed by Kate.

The sale of her father's real estate in 1901 ensured Kate's lifelong financial security and independence. She moved to Melbourne with her sister Laura in 1901 and they lived together at a boarding house run by a Mrs. Nevis[94] at 138 Clarendon Street at East Melbourne.[95]

CHAPTER 2
Sojourn In Victoria

The period after the death of her father and her move to Victoria was a watershed in Kate's life. Because her parents were both deceased she no longer had responsibilities to fulfil as an unmarried daughter. Her stepmother had daughters from a previous marriage to take on this role in her life, so Kate was free from family obligations and financially secure for life. Kate was 37 years old and was preparing to settle down to the life of an affluent spinster and to further her interests in music and botany. She became a member of the Field Naturalists Club of Victoria and met Gustav Weindorfer, eleven years her junior. Their meeting and subsequent marriage changed the course of both their lives.

Two Gentlewomen in Victoria

Kate and Laura lived as gentlewomen at a boarding house in East Melbourne and Kate devoted her time to the study of music and the natural sciences.[96] Their social activities consisted largely of visits to the theatre, art galleries and the library in addition to visiting friends.[97] Kate's interest in the natural sciences caused her to nominate for membership of the Field Naturalists Club of Victoria at an ordinary meeting on 13 October 1902 on the proposal of Charles French Sr. and Charles French Jr.[98] She was elected as a member at the meeting of 17 November 1902[99] and became an active Club member.

Involvement with the Field Naturalists Club of Victoria

Women generally did not play a prominent role in the Field Naturalists Club.[100] However during her three years as a member Kate did not appear typical of this. She wrote two articles clearly demonstrating her botanical knowledge for The Victorian Naturalist: 'Excursion to Yan Yean' and 'Notes of a Visit to Mount Roland'.[101] She was co-leader of a Club excursion with junior members[102] and regularly exhibited Victorian and Tasmanian plant and moss specimens, either gathered on Club excursions or selected from her personal collections, at Club meetings.[103] She also exhibited a collection of dried Victorian plant species at the 15th Conversazione of the Field Naturalists Club of Victoria which was held in the Masonic Hall in Melbourne in October 1905.[104] Kate's botanical knowledge was appreciated by excursion participants, one of whom, A.D. Hardy, acknowledged her assistance to him in helping identify botanical specimens collected during an excursion to the Otway Forest from 24 December 1904 until 2 January 1905:

I am indebted to Miss K. Cowle for help in the botanical collections.[105]

Plate 20: Field Naturalists Club of Victoria excursion to Myers Creek, near St. Leonard, Healesville District,Victoria, 25 November 1911. Dr. C.S. Sutton, friend of Gustav Weindorfer is on the extreme right. Photo: Sims Collection (from the library of J.H. Willis)

This help may have been similar to the extensive list of plant species given to Mr. J.A. Kershaw, who wrote a general report of an excursion to Yarra Glen on 2 April 1904, for The Victorian Naturalist:[106]

The botanical results of the day were not striking, but Miss K. Cowle has handed me the following list of plants and shrubs found in bloom:- Loranthus pendulus growing upon Acacia dealbata, Centipeda cunninghami, Isotoma fluviatilis, Mazus pumilio, Tricoryne elatior, Hypoxis glabella, Lythrum hyssopifolia, Hypericum jappnicum, Convolvulus sepium, Helichryum ferrugineum, Brunella vulgaris, Cassinia aculeata, Viola hederacea, V. betonicifolia, the ubiquitous Goodenia ovata, Erythroea australis, and Bursaria spinosa, with the orchids Pterostylis obtusa and Eriochilus autumnalis. Quantities of the graceful Maidenhair Fern, Adiantum oethiopicum, grew in the glens. Seed specimens of Eucalyptus polyanthema, Schauer, were obtained.

Her obvious expertise in the botanical field was the catalyst of her friendship with fellow Club member, Gustav Weindorfer who had joined the Field Naturalists Club of Victoria in November 1901.[107] No doubt her paper, Notes of a Visit to Mount Roland, Tasmania which was read at a Club meeting in August 1903, and later published in the Club journal,[108] was of interest to him and perhaps the mountainous topography of Tasmania struck a chord within him as a migrant from an alpine country living in a developing, foreign city.

Gustav Weindorfer

Weindorfer was born on the 23rd February 1874 at Spittal, Carinthia and was educated at the State Classical High School in Villach, and the Francisco-Josephinum, an agricultural high school, near Vienna, in order to pursue a career in estate management.[109] After graduating in 1892 he worked in various clerical, accounting and sales positions and became involved in pro-German/anti-Catholic politics which caused him to convert from Roman Catholicism to Protestantism.[110] His decision to emigrate came about because he saw no possibility in following his chosen career in Austria,[111] and also as the result of an unhappy love affair.[112] He arrived in Australia on the 13th June 1900. He did not come to Australia to take the position of Chancellor in the Melbourne Austro-Hungarian Consulate[113] but was offered an office job by the Honorary Austro-Hungarian Consul, Mr. C. Pinschoff when he presented his passport to him after his arrival.[114] He was never the "honorary Chancellor" of the Austro-Hungarian Consulate. Dr. G.F.J. Bergman, says that Weindorfer's choice of Australia as his destination was that it was to be a departure point for further travel and exploration into China, Japan and the South Sea Islands.[115]

Weindorfer was very happy in Australia and thoroughly enjoyed his involvement with the Field Naturalists Club of Victoria and other botanical organisations through which he became a well known and respected botanist. However, his professional life as a clerk at the firm Pfaff, Pinschoff and Co.[116] was unsatisfactory and after he failed to secure the position of Government Botanist with the Department of Agriculture in Victoria in 1905 he decided to return home via the East.[117] He sought permission from the Ministry of the Exterior in Vienna to return home on the Austrian-Hungarian warship, S.M.S. Panther, but his application was refused.[118] In the meantime his friendship with Kate had developed and he had lost interest in returning home.

Plate 21a: Gustav Weindorfer
prior to his marriage to Kate.
Photo: Smith family collection.

Plate 21b: Kate Cowle at the
time of her marriage.
Photo: Courtesy E. Graves.

Weindorfer and Kate were a well suited couple. In addition to botany, they shared a love of music with Kate being an accomplished musician and Weindorfer a fine singer.[119] He would often visit Kate and Laura at their boarding house and Bergman quoted Mr. A.D. Hardy, a fellow member of the Field Naturalists Club of Victoria who lived at the same premises, as saying that Weindorfer frequently visited the women and encouraged and helped Kate to name and classify her plant collection. Afterwards Kate would accompany Weindorfer on the piano as he sang from his own sheet music and that, according to Hardy, 'was the beginning of their romance'.[120] By the winter of 1905 they had decided to marry[121] and Kate's brothers Dan and Charles, and Charles' wife Isabel, left

Launceston for Melbourne on the Loongana on Saturday 7 October 1905 to visit Kate and Laura[122] and to meet Gustav.

Return to Tasmania

Although Dan did not say so, I believe that this visit was to ascertain Gustav's suitability as a husband for Kate. Whenever the Cowle men had previously visited Melbourne, it was either for business purposes or to attend Exhibitions, which were prolific during the latter half of the nineteenth century. Whilst in Melbourne they joined Kate and Gustav shopping, visiting the botanical and zoological gardens, the theatre, museum, library and the art gallery. Dan was quite impressed by a play, For England, at the Theatre Royal in which 'real horses [took] part in it 7 on stage at once'.[123] On 12 October Kate, Gustav and Dan walked together in Richmond Park where Gustav expressed his interest in coming to Tasmania to work with Dan in order to 'learn farming'.[124] Weindorfer had quite obviously said this to please his future brother-in-law as his profession was agricultural estate management, which he loved very much[125] and missed considerably when working in Australia.[126] On 17 October Dan agreed that Weindorfer could work for him in Tasmania as his brother-in-law for 15/- per week which Dan could raise or lower, depending on the circumstances.[127]

Plate 22: SS Flora. Photo: Courtesy Mr. Robert Brooks

19

After he and Kate had decided to marry, Weindorfer applied for Australian citizenship and was granted British citizenship, as was the standard procedure for immigrants to Australia at this time, in September 1905.[128] He arrived in Tasmania on Wednesday 8 November, a fine and warm day, aboard the steamer Flora[129] and began farming with Dan at Lauriston. Kate arrived home a fortnight later, also aboard the Flora, and lived with her sister and brother-in-law, Blanche and Stephen Priest, in Devonport until her marriage two months later.

CHAPTER 3
1906 - 1913

Evidence strongly suggests that Kate and Weindorfer's relationship was based on a deep and loving friendship in which both partners were equal and largely independent. They were married in 1906 and from 1910 onwards lived two lives, one as genteel farmers at Kindred and the other as unorthodox pioneers of the Cradle Valley. Their double lives meant that they spent long periods of time apart whilst Weindorfer set up the Waldheim enterprise and Kate managed the farm. She dearly loved Gustav and missed him when he was away but her support of his endeavours was total. Where possible she helped him physically and financially and ensured that as far as was possible every comfort was provided for him and every detail attended to both at the mountain and at home.

Plate 23: Invitation to the Weindorfer Wedding. Courtesy: R. Hadrill

Kate was not a labourer able to fall trees and split shingles for the chalet but she was an excellent home maker and farm manager. Their homes at the mountain and at Kindred were well looked after and comfortable[130] and in addition to managing the farm she planted vegetables, worked in the dairy and helped to look after the dogs and horses. A share farmer took care of the heavier duties. Seasonal planting and harvesting ensured Weindorfer's regular appearance at the farm and allowed them to enjoy a social life with their friends and family. Although she would have liked to have lived permanently in the Valley with her husband at this stage it was not possible. However, she managed to spend long periods there during the course of building Waldheim Chalet and later looking after paying and non-paying guests.[131] Their long term plan was to sell the farm and live at Waldheim.[132]

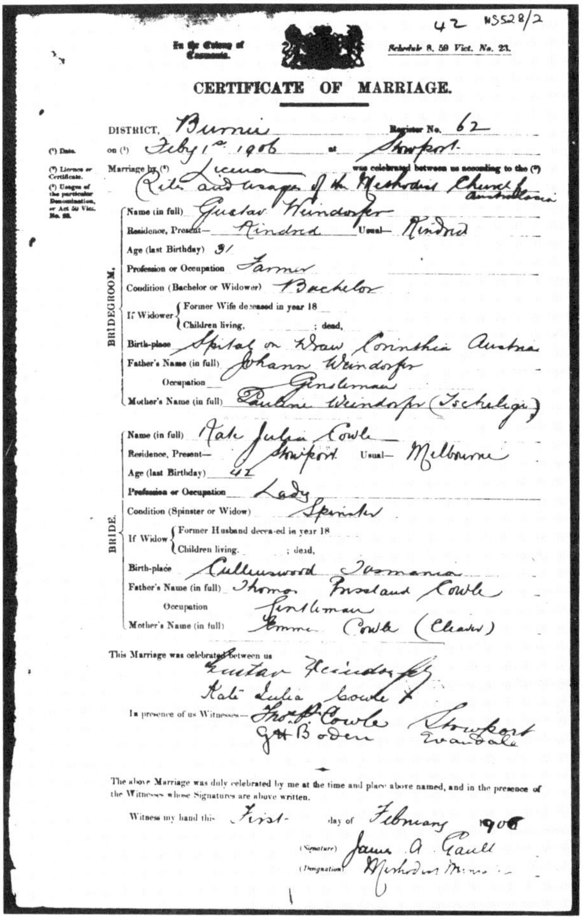

42 MS528/2

In the Colony of Tasmania. Schedule 8, 59 Vict. No. 23.

CERTIFICATE OF MARRIAGE.

DISTRICT, Burnie Register No. 62

(1) Date. on (1) Feby 1st 1906 at Stowport

(2) Licence or Certificate. Marriage by (2) Licence was celebrated between us according to the (3) Rites and usages of the Methodist Church of Australasia

(3) Usages of the particular Denomination, or Act 59 Vict. No. 23.

BRIDEGROOM.

Name (in full) Gustav Weindorfer

Residence, Present— Kindred Usual— Kindred

Age (last Birthday) 31

Profession or Occupation Farmer

Condition (Bachelor or Widower) Bachelor

If Widower { Former Wife deceased in year 18 ; Children living, ; dead,

Birth-place Spital on Drau Corinthia Austria

Father's Name (in full) Johann Weindorfer

Occupation Gentleman

Mother's Name (in full) Pauline Weindorfer (Tschelig)

BRIDE.

Name (in full) Kate Julia Cowle

Residence, Present— Stowport Usual— Melbourne

Age (last Birthday) 42

Profession or Occupation Lady

Condition (Spinster or Widow) Spinster

If Widow { Former Husband deceased in year 18 ; Children living, ; dead,

Birth-place Culleswood Tasmania

Father's Name (in full) Thomas Freeland Cowle

Occupation Gentleman

Mother's Name (in full) Emma Cowle (Clarke)

This Marriage was celebrated between us Gustav Weindorfer
Kate Julia Cowle

In presence of us Witnesses— Thos F Cowle Stowport
G H Boden Evandale

The above Marriage was duly celebrated by me at the time and place above named, and in the presence of the Witnesses whose Signatures are above written.

Witness my hand this First day of February 1906

(Signature) James A Gault

(Designation) Methodist Minister

Plate 24: The Weindorfers marriage certificate.
Photo: Courtesy Tasmanian State Archives.

Wedding at Stowport

Prior to her wedding Kate left her temporary home in Devonport with her sister and brother-in-law Blanche and Stephen Priest to live with her brother Press and his wife Eva at their farm, Killara, at Stowport near Burnie. Press was the eldest son of the Cowle family and consequently held the role of patriarch as a result of his father's death twelve years earlier. He was to perform the traditional task of giving the bride away. Kate spent her last days as a single woman attending to last minute details of the wedding and honeymoon. In a hurried letter to her sister Blanche the day before her wedding Kate reveals her excitement at the prospect ahead. The short sharp sentences are unlike her usual structured and conversational style and the spontaneous reference to Gustav's arrival with her brother Dan indicates her delight at seeing him again:

Dear Blanche

We cannot get through to Sheffield on the Friday, so would you mind if we stay Friday night with you. we [sic] could both sleep in my little room [and] in Gustav's bed - [and] go on by the morning train to Sheffield. G. [and] Dan have just arrived. So sorry you are not coming - The cake is very pretty - Hope all are well - Fearful hurry - Love from Kate -

We will come along by the afternoon train on Friday to Devonport - [133]

Kate and Gustav were to be married at 3.00pm on Thursday 1 February 1906 in the Stowport Church[134] but a bushfire the previous day and night had destroyed it. The fire seriously threatened Killara, forcing wedding guests and family, including Weindorfer,[135] to fight to contain it. The loss of the Church caused a last minute change of venue and a time delay, and they were eventually married in Press and Eva's drawing room at 3.30pm[136] by the Methodist Minister, James A. Gault.[137] Kate was 42, almost 11 years older than her husband. The couple left Killara at 5.30pm for Penguin where they stayed overnight at Watcombe House.[138] Dan joined them at 9am the following morning and they left Penguin together for Devonport where Kate and Gustav stayed overnight at Lenna[139] prior to setting out for Sheffield the following day.

Plate 25: Kate's brother, Press Cowle, and his family. Left to right: Eva, Dorothy, Press and Violet. Photo: Courtesy R. Hadrill.

Plate 26: Lenna, The Priest family home in Devonport where Kate lived prior to her marriage. Photo: Courtesy R. Hadrill.

Mt. Roland Honeymoon

Kate and Gustav left Devonport by train on Saturday 3 February[140] to commence a five week honeymoon on Mount Roland, behind Sheffield, where they intended to collect plant

24

species of the area.[141] They caught O'Grady's Coach, driven by Lyndon George Bramich,[142] at Railton and arrived in Sheffield at 11am where they bought supplies in readiness for their honeymoon camp.[143] They stayed overnight at the Perkins family farm at the foot of Mount Roland and earlier in the day Dick Perkins took Gustav to the campsite to store some supplies.[144] It is possible that this was a well established campsite used regularly by the Perkins men for hunting trips on the mountain. The following morning the Perkins' boys and their father accompanied the Weindorfers' to the camp, helping carry the remaining supplies. They left their dog Brit with Kate and Gustav for company.[145]

During their time on the mountain the Weindorfers encountered all types of hazards including temperature extremes, rain, thunder and lightning, bushfires and mosquitoes.[146] However the weather was mostly fine and they spent their days collecting plant specimens, exploring the mountain and hunting kangaroo for fresh meat. Their evenings were spent cooking their meal and sorting and pressing their specimens after which they would play the violin and flute.

Plate 27: Mt Roland postcard, 1906. Courtesy Sims Collection.

Their unusual choice of honeymoon location caused great interest amongst the local people. To satisfy their curiosity Kate and Gustav wrote a series of letters in a humorous brogue using the pseudonyms, Pat Heggarty and Mike

O'Flannagan, to the local newspapers the North Western Advocate and Emu Bay Times on their return to Devonport. The letters are quite revealing in that they allow the reader to gain an insight into the Weindorfers' close and companionable relationship. They reveal their hobbies, hopes for the future and daily life at the campsite: A 'sly glance' by 'Pat' into their tent revealed a 'bed looking like a comfortable couch'.[147] Gustav left the mountain twice a week from the mountain to 'replenish their larder' which was well stocked with 'cherries [and] strawberries as well as 'honey [and] onions'.[148] Their 'tucker bags' held 'three hams, case o' jam tins, half [a hundredweight] o' taters, three frying pans, six billies and other little things.'[149] They put these items to good use according to 'Mike': 'making all sorts o' dishes'.[150] After dinner they catalogued their 'bulging knapsacks'[151] of plant species collected during the day. On completion of their tasks 'the swate tones of a fiddle and a flute' drifted through the mountain air leaving 'Mike' quite broken up but knowing that Kate and Gustav were able to 'find happiness even in "sterile regions."'[152] But it was the statement: 'Sure there's no tellin' pwhat nixt, for Roland may be only a shtep to Mt. 'Wellington', to be followed by 'Cradle' Mountain'[153] that intentionally, or unintentionally, revealed their future plans.

Plate 28: The Hanging Rock, geomorphic feature of Mount Roland. Courtesy Sims Collection.

On their return to Devonport Kate bought 100 acres of farm-land at Kindred from her brother, Dan Cowle. She was the most affluent of the couple as a result of having been well provided for by her late father. Roland Lea was part of the original Cowle family farm, Lauriston, and was purchased in May 1906 for £15/10/0 per acre[154] after considerable haggling with Dan.

Establishing Roland Lea

Kate's capital was put to use to build a new home for the couple. Their home was kept neat and uncluttered[155] and was no doubt a welcome change from the original rundown cottage on the property in which they lived whilst the new house was being built.[156] They jointly managed the farm and employed help only as required. Gustav's profession as an Estate Manager in Austria proved to be valuable and he applied his knowledge of modern farming practices at Roland Lea with great success. An orchard was laid out, sheep and cattle purchased, a dairy installed and vegetables and grain were sown using seed imported from Germany.[157] The quality of the produce was such that Gustav earned respect and admiration from local farmers and recognition from the Hobart Agricultural Council.[158]

Kate and Gustav settled happily into marriage and life as farmers. They were considered upper class by the local residents although they treated all people kindly regardless of their social ranking.[159] Kate's sister Laura was a regular visitor to Roland Lea as were her sister and brother-in-law Blanche and Stephen Priest and their children. Stephen was an architect and he and Gustav became friends. They were the same age and were both migrants with Stephen being born in Canada[160] and until Gustav's death in 1932 they regularly visited one another and Gustav would always stay at Lenna whenever he was in Devonport.[161]

Family events were held at Lauriston and on one occasion Stephen had designed and built a caravan which was immensely enjoyed by the Cowle and Priest children at the time. Kate and Gustav had made friends with a neighbour Ronald Edgar Smith and his fiancee Kathleen Carruthers. Ronie [sic] as he was known to his friends, would join them on botanical rambles[162] and together they developed an interested in photography and film processing.[163] He was an avid supporter of Gustav and Kate's Cradle Mountain enterprise and with his wife was a regular visitor.

Plate 29:Roland Lea, Kate and Gustav's house at Kindred.
Photo: Courtesy Craig Broadfield and the Ulverstone History Museum.

During the establishment of the Cradle Mountain venture various share farmers, including a Mr. Rodgers and a Mr. Bramich,[164] were later employed by the Weindorfer's to help Kate manage Roland Lea and to run it entirely during the absence of them both. During her time alone at the farm Kate worked in the dairy separating cream from milk and making butter. She maintained her kitchen garden and weeded and planted vegetables, organised the household and attended to any business matters that might arise. She looked after the dogs and horses, feeding them each night and morning and paid the wages of casual workers and the share farmer. She was generally responsible for managing the couples' finances and acted as guarantor for loans and bank overdrafts for Gustav when necessary. This sometimes caused problems because his frequent absences resulted in banks and creditors wanting payment of overdrafts and accounts with the occasional threat of Court action to recover debts.[165]

Plate 30: Family occasion at Lauriston. Kate is standing to the right of Gustav, who is holding baby Charles Priest. Photo: Courtesy R. Hadrill.

On the completion of their house in 1907 and after they had settled in Kate and Gustav invited his parents to spend a holiday with them.[166] The old couple were very excited about this and looked forward to seeing their son again and meeting their daughter-in-law of whom they had grown very fond.[167] They arrived in February 1908 and immediately made friends with Kate and her family and Mr. Weindorfer became very popular in the district, especially with young Florence Trebilco.[168] Flossie, as she was known, was a gifted pianist and Johann Weindorfer wanted her to return to Europe with him and his wife, Pauline, where he was convinced that she was capable of becoming a noted concert pianist.[169] The arrival of his parents gave Gustav the freedom to leave the farm and make his first visit to Cradle Mountain which he climbed with his Melbourne friend Dr. Sutton in January 1909.[170] He later described Cradle Valley as 'veritable flower garden, a true El Dorado for the botanist, and a magnificent place for the tourist'.[171] On his return home his excitement about the botanical opportunities offered there enthused Kate and on December 28 of the same year she accompanied Gustav and their friend and neighbour Ronald Smith into Cradle Valley.[172]

Because of inclement weather they stayed at the Middlesex cattle station until 31 December[173] and accompanied by a Mr

Perry and two pack horses set out for Cradle Valley and their campsite, a newly built hut at Fiery galena mine at the foot of Mt. Remus owned by Mr W. Black who briefly joined them the following day.[174] The hut was too far away from Cradle Mountain to use as a permanent base so the Weindorfers and Ronald Smith moved further into the Valley and established a campsite at Crater Lake on 3 January intending to stay for one week.[175] On 4 January the party left camp at 7am and climbed Cradle Mountain collecting plant species along the way. Kate, resplendent in a large hat and whalebone corset beneath a billowing dress, achieved the honour of being the first recorded woman to climb Cradle Mountain. It was from the summit on this day that Weindorfer made his famous statement:

This must be a National Park for the people for all time. It is magnificent, and people must know about it and enjoy it.[176]

Plate 31: Climbing Cradle Mountain in 1911.
Top to Bottom: Dr Sutton, Kate, Kathleen Carruthers, Gustav.
Photo: Smith Family Collection.

30

On the summit the possibilities of establishing a tourist venture and having the area declared a National Park were discussed. The plan was simple. The Weindorfers' would build a home at the mountain and when visitors began arriving and the venture proved to be a success, the Government would build a road into the area, similar to the Buffalo Mountains project in Victoria of which they were both familiar.[177] Their enthusiasm was such that when they descended the mountain, they selected the site for their chalet on the north-west side of the Valley near two creeks.[178] They stayed in the Valley exploring the Cradle Mountain cirque with its myriad of lakes and forests, collecting plants, mosses and lichens until 10 January when rain prompted a move back to Mr Black's hut.[179] Ronald Smith returned home at this point and the Weindorfers spent the following three days exploring and adding to their specimen portfolio, before leaving the Valley on the 14th.[180]

Establishing the Cradle Mountain Venture:

At this time Cradle Valley was classified as third class Crown land and was being logged by individuals and the Gordon Timber Company.[181] In order to protect as much of the area as they could, the Weindorfers and Smiths decided to buy the maximum acreage permitted. On their return to Kindred from their first visit to Cradle Valley Kate and Gustav immediately began to make inquiries about purchasing land in the Valley and returned there with Ronald Smith to survey the land they wished to buy.[182] On payment of a survey fee of £14/0/0 to the Secretary for Lands on 16 October 1910[183] and a deposit of £2/0/0 to the State Treasury Kate's 200 acreage was secured on 25 April 1911.[184] Gustav, Ronald Smith and his mother had previously each bought 200 acres of land with boundaries adjoining Kate's in 1910 and in later years the Smiths purchased further acreage increasing their holding to 1200 acres.[185]

Many happy times were spent together in the Valley, initially in tents and then in the chalet, developing their tourism venture whilst Weindorfer kept meteorological records for the Bureau of Meteorology and trapped native animals for fresh meat for themselves and their dogs. The animal skins were sold to local skin merchants and Kate would take the uncured skins back to the farm where she aired them daily in order that they be in prime condition ready for sale.[186] Kate joined Gustav regularly during the course of building Waldheim and later looking after paying and non-paying guests who would be taken bushwalking, mountaineering or skiing, depending on weather conditions.

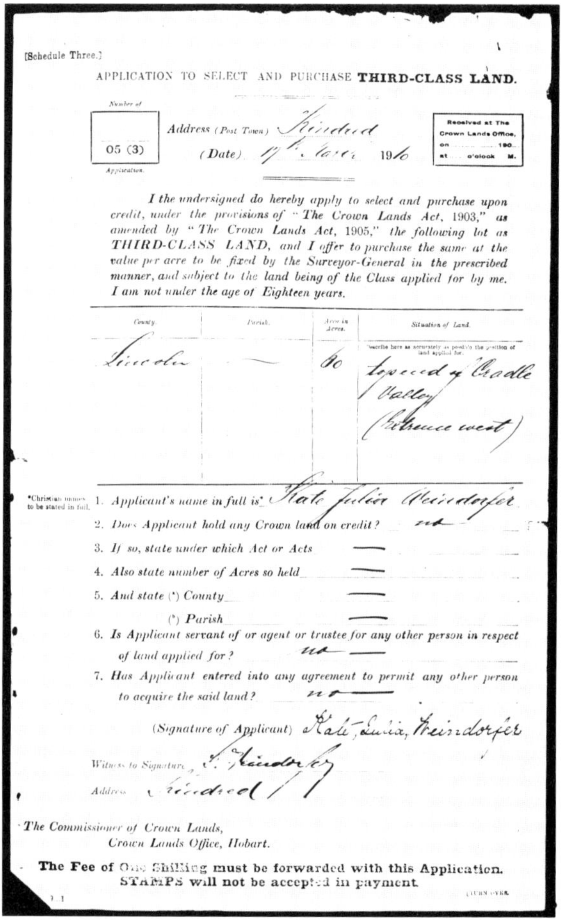

[Schedule Three.]

APPLICATION TO SELECT AND PURCHASE **THIRD-CLASS LAND.**

Number of Application: 05 (3)

Address (Post Town) Kindred

(Date) 17th Mar 1910

Received at The Crown Lands Office, on .... 190.. at .... o'clock M.

I the undersigned do hereby apply to select and purchase upon credit, under the provisions of "The Crown Lands Act, 1903," as amended by "The Crown Lands Act, 1905," the following lot as THIRD-CLASS LAND, and I offer to purchase the same at the value per acre to be fixed by the Surveyor-General in the prescribed manner, and subject to the land being of the Class applied for by me. I am not under the age of Eighteen years.

County.	Parish.	Area in Acres.	Situation of Land. (Describe here as accurately as possible the position of land applied for.)
Lincoln	—	60	topend of Cradle Valley (Entrance west)

*Christian names to be stated in full.

1. *Applicant's name in full is* Kate Julia Weindorfer
2. *Does Applicant hold any Crown land on credit?* no
3. *If so, state under which Act or Acts* —
4. *Also state number of Acres so held* —
5. *And state (*) County* —
   (*) Parish —
6. *Is Applicant servant of or agent or trustee for any other person in respect of land applied for?* no
7. *Has Applicant entered into any agreement to permit any other person to acquire the said land?* no

(Signature of Applicant) Kate Julia Weindorfer

Witness to Signature G. Weindorfer

Address Kindred

The Commissioner of Crown Lands,
Crown Lands Office, Hobart.

The Fee of One Shilling must be forwarded with this Application. STAMPS will not be accepted in payment

(TURN OVER.

Plate 32: Application by Kate to purchase land at Cradle Valley.
Photo: Local History Museum, Launceston.

Plate 33: Camp at Looseleaf Creek 1911, close to location of Waldheim Chalet.
Left to right: Kathleen Carruthers, Kate, Ronald Smith, Gustav, C.S. Sutton.
Photo: Smith Family Collection.

Weindorfer designed Waldheim, meaning home in the forest, in the style of Austrian mountain chalets. He began to build it on Kate's acreage in March 1912.[187] Although the chalet was not completely finished it was sufficiently so to accept paying guests by Christmas of the same year.[188] Kate and Gustav's personal friends spent numerous happy times with them at the mountain and unless they absolutely insisted on paying the Weindorfers waived costs.[189] The chalet was built from King Billy pine selectively chosen by Gustav from the forest. A local splitter, Dennison, was employed to help fell and split the logs for building the chalet and for fencing purposes.[190] The pine was not always suitable for splitting and occasionally myrtle was used.[191] By 1913 the chalet was well underway with Dennison splitting palings whilst Weindorfer worked on the framework, ceilings, walls and floors and hanging windows.[192]

Kate's letters kept him in touch with all that was happening in Kindred and Devonport. She loved Weindorfer and missed him very much, and spent many hours writing letters to him and reading and rereading his replies. Her letters to him were full of every day events on the farm and of family news. They contained anecdotes which must have cheered Weindorfer after a hard days work at the mountain. She quotes 'Tib', their share farmer as telling her 'the oats in the long paddock are "coming on something lovely"',[193] and relates how their dog Bixie was disgraced for eating the lunches out of the children's' bags at the schoolhouse next door to Roland Lea.[194] Her pride in the success of his first attempt at cake making is evident in her letter to him of 11 August 1913: 'my dear boy's brownie was a success. I am so glad. Will you be trying a beefsteak pudding?'. She did not attempt to hide her longing for him, particularly on days when she was feeling lonely. She writes how she wept on receiving his letters and how she missed her 'dear boy'[195] and was 'hungry' to hear from him and to see him again.[196] When Flock, their female dog, was allowed to smell his letter 'she licked it all over, she could evidently smell you'.[197] Flock was a comfort to Kate: 'I should be lonely without her, it is nice to feel there is some living thing full of affection to welcome me in the morning and follow me all day.'[198]

Plate 34: Waldheim Chalet in summer. Postcard: Sims Collection.

Her time alone at the farm was broken with regular visits to Waldheim. One of these was a six and a half week stay from June 13 to 29 July 1913. Because of wet and cold weather conditions much of this time was spent working on the chalet. Weindorfer built the verandah, chimney and spouting on the chalet's exterior and a kennel for their dogs. Inside he built food shelves, bedroom doors and floors, the mantle piece and his big easy chair. Later a second chair was built for Kate. When the weather improved they explored the area together and hunted for dog food.[199] On 19 July Kate celebrated her 50th birthday at Waldheim.

Plate 35: Kate and Gustav. Photo: Courtesy Craig Broadfield and the Ulverstone History Museum.

Kate was a courageous woman who was unafraid to face hardship head on. On her return to Kindred from this visit she was driving alone in the cart pulled by Gustav's horse Jolly when she encountered a raging storm. She caught up with the Singer Sewing Machines traveller who was very frightened and they joined forces to negotiate fallen trees and other storm debris on the road, pulling down a fence at one point to enable them to pass. Gale force winds and rain accompanied them down Gentle Annie Hill to Wilmot where they parted company. Kate continued through the storm to Forth where she stayed overnight with Ronald Smith's wife and mother, Kathie and Mrs Smith.[200] This courage was to serve her well during her drawn out and painful death less than three years later.

Plate 36: Waldheim Chalet in winter.
Photo: Courtesy Tasmanian State Archives.

A three week visit was made in September 1913 which she had been looking forward to.[201] She purchased carbide and nails and supplies of flour and other non-perishable items, cooked and gathered fresh vegetables from their garden to take to Gustav.[202] During her stay he built the big window table[203] at which he used to sit alone and in the dark after Kate's death and when he had no visitors and wait for the animals to come in to share the warmth of his fire.[204]

By 1913 Waldheim was well established as a tourist destination and was being promoted by the Northern Tasmania Tourist Association.[205] In their promotional material the Weindorfers described it as an ideal holiday resort where tourists and holiday makers could bushwalk, climb mountains, fish, shoot and skate and ski in the winter. The chalet provided comfortable accommodation and was 'the last word in luxury' considering the impossibility of bringing in any quantity of building materials.[206] They described the district as of remarkable interest to the geologist, scientist and naturalist but visitors were warned that it was not the place for those expecting to laze around in easy chairs with books and iced drinks![207]

Board and lodging cost 8/- per day and 10/- for an employed guide.[208]

*Plate 37: Waldheim Chalet with Cradle Mountain
in the background through the trees, about 1912.
Photo: Courtesy Tasmanian State Archives.*

Visitors reached the Valley by rail to Devonport/Sheffield or Ulverstone/Forth and then by road to Wilmot, the Middlesex Plains and Cradle Valley where they were met by Weindorfer at Pencil Pine river. A limit of 200 lbs. was placed on luggage because through lack of a suitable road from this point visitors were charged 10/- per trip with 1d. per additional pound of luggage over 200 lbs.[209] Visitors left with glowing accounts of the Weindorfers' hospitality and of the beautiful scenery of Cradle Mountain, but not all people were satisfied. A surveyor, F. Wilks, B.C.E., complained of the costs involved with his stay early in 1914 because he believed the trip was solely for his convenience and was annoyed that Weindorfer carted some of his own baggage in.[210] He felt that the transport and meal costs were astonishing and proffered a word of advice to Weindorfer that he was making a great mistake at placing his charges so high to local residents who could, with less cost and a little inconvenience, provide better for themselves! He warned Weindorfer that his extortionate charges would soon kill the business with local people,[211] a warning that proved to be quite unfounded.

Plate 38: Gustav Weindorfer at Cradle Mountain.
Photo: Courtesy Mrs Dorothy Filgate.

The first seven years of Kate's married life were filled with adventure and happiness. Meeting Weindorfer had completely changed the course of both their lives. Prior to their meeting she was settling down to a life as a learned spinster and he was unsettled, disenchanted and ready to leave Australia. Weindorfer released the dormant adventuress in Kate and she gave him the freedom and means to satisfy his restless spirit and realise his dreams in return. Neither would have or could have accomplished alone that which they did together. Sadly they were to have less than three more years together and ironically it was the success of the Cradle Mountain enterprise that separated them at a time when she needed him most.

CHAPTER 4
1914-1916

Kate did not spend a great deal of time at the mountain during the final two years of her life. A large percentage of her
time was spent consulting doctors about her declining health
which necessitated many visits to Ulverstone, Devonport and
Launceston. Weindorfer was absent for long periods of time at
Cradle Mountain acting as host and guide to their many visitors there. Kate was a practical woman and well aware that the
enterprise, along with the farm, provided part of their income
as well as being the source of great pleasure to them both. As
her health began to deteriorate she was unable to join him as
often as she would have liked. Her letters to him express her
longing for his companionship but she never suggested that he
should abandon the undertaking or hire a guide to care for the
visitors and come home to her.

Peace in the Valley

Kate and Gustav were well established by 1914 and on 5
May they travelled to Devonport to make enquiries about sell-
ing the farm[212] in order to live permanently at the mountain.
On the same day they purchased a gas stove[213] which was later
to be a source of trouble for Weindorfer when it was reported
to the government as 'heavy machinery' during the 'spy scare'
period of World War I.[214] He made a quick trip into the Valley
to install it and because of its size and weight he and a friend
were forced to dismantle it and carry it in on a stretcher.[215]
Waldheim was now completed and needed only finishing
touches[216] such as the installation of drains for it to be truly
home.[217] They had arranged to rent Roland Lea to a share
farmer, Mr. Rodgers, for £80/0/0 a year and by the end of May
the Rodgers family had settled into the farm cottage.[218] Mrs
Rodgers is said to have been untidy and the children were
blamed for infecting the entire Kindred school with lice![219] But
for all that Mr Rodgers was a good farmer and Roland Lea continued to prosper. The local school teacher, Miss Stephenson,
agreed to live in their house during their absences[220] which
proved to be convenient for both parties as the Weindorfers

could rest easy at the mountain knowing their home was well cared for and Miss Stevenson was able to reside next door to the school house.

Business matters were settled in Ulverstone and Devonport and supplies were purchased to enable them to return to the Valley to spend the winter of 1914. They arrived on 7 June and remained until 11 September.[221] Although she visited the mountain on and off for the rest of 1914, this was Kate's last extended stay in the Valley. When war was declared between the Allies and Germany in August 1914 Kate and Gustav were established at Waldheim for the winter and the miseries of war were remote from them. Neither of them were to know then the damaging impact it was later to have on Weindorfer. In a letter to her parents-in-law in August 1914, which was never posted, Kate wrote:

> ... Here in the solitude and solemn peace of the majestic mountains, it is impossible to realise that war is raging on the other side of the world... outside the snow is thickly on the ground, but a fine fire of logs burns in the big fireplace, [and] little Flock lies in front on the wombat rug peacefully asleep ...[222]

Plate 39: Cradle Mountain reflected in Lake Lilla.
Postcard: Courtesy John Clayton.

Health Problems

It was on the June-September 1914 visit to the Valley that Kate first experienced the health problems which were to continue

40

for the rest of her life. Entries in Weindorfer's diaries relate how she was 'indisposed' and spent several full days in bed.[223] She was kept awake all of one night with chest pains and on their return home she visited Dr. Gollan in Ulverstone who diagnosed her condition as 'acute indigestion'.[224] Local women from Kindred were employed to manage the household affairs for her, including twelve year old Phyllis Granger who worked for Kate one morning a week until her death and remembers her with affection. Kate continued to visit Cradle Mountain but did not stay as long as she had previously. Her final visit was in June 1915.[225] Weindorfer was very concerned about her and did not spend as much time there as before, staying for days instead of months and going only when required as a guide for tourist groups or when Kate's condition appeared to improve.[226]

Plate 40: Kate painting at Kindred with her maid Phyllis Granger.
Photo: Ulverstone History Museum.

By 1915 Kate's health had seriously deteriorated and many visits were made to doctors and hospitals in Ulverstone, Devonport and Launceston. The state of her health fluctuated. When she felt well she worked around the farm caring for the garden, chickens, dogs and horses, attending to business matters[227] and arranging details of visitors bound for Waldheim.[228] By October she was quite weak and suffered debilitating pain and was no longer able to tend her garden which she had enjoyed doing.[229] She spent a considerable amount of time in Devonport staying at Lenna where Blanche and Laura cared for her. In spite of feeling homesick and missing Weindorfer she enjoyed the company of her young nieces, Laura and Kathleen Priest, and spent time on the beach in the sunshine with them.[230]

Plate 41:Kate's sister and brother in-law Blanche and Stephen Priest and their children. Left to right: Stephen nursing Press, Laura, Blanche and Kathleen. Photo: Courtesy R. Hadrill.

The local women enjoyed her company and Kate was invited to four 'afternoons' held in her honour which she enjoyed immensely.[231] The women entertained themselves chatting, knitting, playing and singing and Kate modestly informed Weindorfer that 'If I were vain I should feel quite a "personage" down here'.[232] Whilst she was in Devonport her doctor, Dr. Payne, found a lump in her left breast which Dr. Gollan had diagnosed as an enlarged muscle.[233] However, Dr. Payne asserted that her condition was the result of angina pectoris and high blood pressure[234] which he reaffirmed at the end of the year:

'...Dr Payne told her, her hart [sic] is bad.'[235]

42

Plate 42: Kate with her sisters and nephews. Left to right: Blanche Priest holding her son Charles, Kate, Press Priest, Laura Cowle, maid. This is possibly the last photograph taken of Kate. Photo: Courtesy R. Hadrill.

Plate 43: Matron Lucy Moreton's Hospital at Ulverstone. Photo: Courtesy Ulverstone History Museum.

Dr Payne referred Kate to Dr. Sweetman in Launceston to have the lump x-rayed[236] in order that it be treated. She travelled there by train in November 1915 accompanied by her sister Laura. The x-rays did not reveal any problem[237] but one must be aware that x-ray results were not always accurate then. Her doctor ordered absolute rest[238] which she ignored, choosing instead to visit the Tourist Bureau to find out whether they were sufficiently promoting Waldheim Chalet to tourists![239] In December Weindorfer took several tourist groups to the mountain and returned on the 14th to discover Kate had been admitted to Matron Lucy Moreton's private hospital in Ulverstone with heart and lung problems.[240] She was very thin and weak and was unable to write to him, probably as a result of being given morphine injections for pain relief,[241] leaving it to Laura to do for her.[242] Gustav's concern for Kate is evident by the almost daily entries in his diary concerning her health and activities. He would bike regularly into Ulverstone to visit her, once three times in the same day.[243]

Her health appeared to improve at the beginning of 1916 and Kate was allowed home from Hospital. Secure in the knowledge that she was being well cared for by Laura,[244] Weindorfer took a tourist group into the mountain late in January. However the day after his return home on 5 February she was very ill and was taken to Dr. Gollan's house in Ulverstone from where she was driven to Matron Moreton's hospital the same day by Weindorfer in Dr. Gollan's motor car.[245] She did not come home again. On 18 March Weindorfer was committed to take a party of three gentlemen into Cradle Mountain and on the 22nd he found a note from Mr. Hitchcock from Wilmot:

> Dear Mr. Weindorfer'
>
> I was called up on telephone this morning at noon from Ulverstone. There was a very great difficulty in hearing but what I could make out was that you were wanted as soon as possible. I could not catch the name of the speaker exactly it seemed to be Powell or Cowell. He said either that Mrs. Weindorfer was no worse or was worse (I could not distinguish which) but that you were wanted as soon as possible. If anything it seemed as if he said Mrs. Weindorfer is no worse I trust this is so I am sending a messenger to the station with instructions that if they cannot send you word to go on himself.
>
> Yours faithfully
>
> Wm. Hitchcock[246]

Kate's health deteriorated rapidly and on the 27th April Gustav sadly records in his diary that 'Kate realises the hopelessness of her state.'[247] On the 29th April 1916 on a glorious Autumn day, Kate died at 1.20pm and Gustav lost his best friend.[248] She was not quite 53 years old and they had been married for 10 short but happy years. Although her death certificate states that she died from chronic nephritis and uraemia,[249] she had been diagnosed with a series of complaints ranging from heart disease through to indigestion. However, the lump found by Dr. Payne in her breast in 1915 should not be overlooked as it is quite possible that her painful and drawn out death was the result of breast cancer. We will never know the true cause of her death.

Kate had remained in control of her life until the very end. On 25 March Gustav had spent the day at her bedside[250] and on that day she added a Codicil to her Will. It was hand written and signed by Matron Moreton and Nurse Sylvia Dawes. In it she instructed her trustees, one of whom was Gustav, to sell the farm and to 'pay the means to my said husband during his life.'[251] Except for a few minor bequests listed in her Will and written on a separate list enclosed with it she left her holding at Cradle Mountain and all of her remaining goods and chattels unconditionally to Weindorfer.[252] By altering her Will as she did, Kate ensured that he had sanctuary in the home he loved best at Cradle Mountain and a considerable sum of money to cover any needs he may have had. The capital value of the farm in 1916 was £1,449/0/0[253] but it was not sold until 1926.[254] This may have been because some members of her family believed that legally it was unlikely that he would be able to own title to the properties because he was viewed as a subject of an enemy nation.[255]

Her death was a blow to all who knew her, and especially to Weindorfer. He was in an untenable position after her death and in the same year he lost most of his family - Kate, both his parents and his brother Lothar.[256] He was under considerable stress as a result of anti-German sentiment directed at him as a result of World War I and heightened by heavy losses incurred at Gallipoli.[257] Locals accused him of being pro-German and a spy[258] and some of Kate's family blamed him for her death, believing that the long periods she spent at the mountain had been detrimental to her health.[259] After losing Kate, Weindorfer had no reason to remain at Kindred and moved permanently to Cradle Mountain.

Plate 44: Weindorfer. Photo: Courtesy Tasmanian State Archives.

CHAPTER 5
Conclusion

Although I have intentionally not researched Kate Weindorfer from a feminist perspective, the study of her does raise feminist issues. These include the role of women generally and feminist methodology in history research. Kate's role in the Cradle Mountain venture has been well documented in this paper and with respect to feminist methodology in history research I believe that it was unnecessary to employ special concepts to tell her story because abundant primary sources of information are available proving she is definitely not a token woman added to the Cradle Mountain legend.

With regard to the role of women generally, by early twentieth century standards Kate Weindorfer was unique. She was well educated and her interest in bushwalking and botany was developed long before she met Weindorfer as is evidenced by her article Notes of a Visit to Mount Roland, Tasmania[260] and from family photographs. In other respects she was very much a woman of her time in that until she was 38 years old she was the typical 'spinster aunt' available to her extended family as a companion and carer. However the financial independence she acquired on the settlement of her father's estate in 1901 caused her to break this cycle by moving to Melbourne to further her interests in music and botany.

I believe that her meeting Weindorfer in 1902 was a meeting of kindred spirits which changed the course of both their lives. Until this time Kate had settled into a single and academic life and Weindorfer was unsettled with a strong desire to return home and to his profession as an estate manager. After their marriage they had planned to settle down to a quiet farming life on Roland Lea at Kindred but Weindorfers first sight of Tasmania's magnificent mountain ranges from the summit of Mount Roland on their honeymoon evoked memories of Austria and the potential for developing the concept of wilderness holidays in this state, similar to that which was occurring in his homeland, was born. It was Weindorfer's vision of what could be achieved and Kate's total support of him combined with their mutual love of natural sciences that was the catalyst of the formation of the Cradle Mountain Reserve. After Weindorfers death this was merged with the Lake St. Clair Reserve, forming the Cradle Mountain-Lake St. Clair National Park as we know it today.

Plate 45: Kate with her brothers and sisters. Left to right: Dan, Blanche, Charles, Bert and Kate Cowle. This photograph was probably taken at Lauriston, towards the Forth River. Photo: Courtesy R. Hadrill.

Is Kate an 'added woman' in the Cradle Mountain legend? I believe not. Kate played definite roles in the Cradle Mountain venture and these are supported by evidence found in personal letters and diaries, receipts of land purchases and legal documents. Her comfortable financial position was such that she was able to purchase their farm which ensured an income to support them and pay expenses during the establishment of the venture. The employment of a share farmer under Kate's management gave Weindorfer the freedom to spend as much time as was needed at Cradle Valley, initially to build the chalet and later to act as guide and host to paying guests and friends.

Kate regularly spent time at the mountain ranging from short visits to extended stays of several months during which time she would care and cook for guests and take parties on less arduous bushwalks to areas such as Wombat Pool.[261] In the earlier years during the building of Waldheim she was unable to physically do what Weindorfer did at the mountain or on the

48

farm. Her role then was that of a business manager, wife and friend, attending to business matters concerning the farm and the mountain venture, caring for Weindorfer by taking care of his comforts, preparing his meals and helping out where possible both on the farm and at the mountain. He enjoyed her company and the times they spent together at Waldheim and although he rarely stated personal feelings in his diaries there are entries revealing that when she was back at the farm it was quiet and lonely without her: 'camp dull and lonely after Kate gone.'[262] There is no doubt that he loved her and considered her to be his best friend.[263] An anecdote told to me by Mrs Filgate of Beauty Point tells the story of the first meeting between her mother, Mrs Lucy King, and Weindorfer long after Kate's death. Mrs King was 'a young wife of approximately 12 months, [who had experienced] a very strict and Christian upbringing [she] ... was taken by "Dorfer" who said "You come with me." She went, feeling very apprehensive. She was taken into his bedroom where he picked up a photo and showed it to her saying "This was my wife."[264] Evidence proves that Kate could never be considered as an 'added woman' in Weindorfer's life or in the Cradle Mountain endeavour. Her total support of him and commitment to his dream combined with her efficient management of other aspects of their lives gave Weindorfer total freedom to establish Cradle Valley as a reserve for all people and ensured the success of the venture.

Without Kate's involvement in Weindorfer's life it is doubtful that the Cradle Mountain-Lake St. Clair National Park as we know it would be a reality today. The obvious reason is that had he not met her, based on available evidence it is plausible to suggest that he may have returned to Austria and may never have came to Tasmania and it is unlikely that a different person would have had his vision and commitment to realise the potential of the area. In view of her commitment to the project one must ask why has Kate been overlooked for so many years? It is my belief that this has occurred as a result of three factors. I believe that Kate's lingering illness and eventual death in 1916 was primarily the cause. By 1912 Waldheim chalet was completed and visitors were beginning to enter and enjoy the Valley and the company of the Weindorfers but by

1914 Kate's health began to deteriorate and World War I was declared.

Her illness meant that she was unable to spend as much time as before at the mountain and by 1915 she was experiencing considerable pain and discomfort requiring many visits to doctors and hospitals. She was physically unable to travel great distances or to stay at the mountain for the same periods of time and as a result Gustav was forced to assume full responsibility for guests.

World War I was the second factor. It restricted the numbers of visitors into the Valley as a result of the war effort and constraints which meant that only reasonably well off people could make the trip. The anti-German feeling directed towards Weindorfer no doubt did not help but it is unlikely to have been a major factor. After Kate's death in 1916 Weindorfer made Cradle Mountain his permanent home and until the end of the War his visitors were generally his personal friends. These lonely years created the foundations of the hermit/lone man legend and when the War ended in 1919 and the mountain came into its own as a popular tourist destination in the 1920s Kate was no longer a part of it. Many of the new visitors to the mountain had never met her and knew nothing about her. In fact many people to this day do not realise that Weindorfer had even married.

It was not until after Weindorfer's death on 5 May 1932 that a series of events occurred that inadvertently reinforced the hermit/lone man legend which pushed Kate further into the background. In November 1932, his sister, Rosa Moritsch, sent everlasting flowers and four candles to Tasmania with the request that they be placed on her brother's grave at Christmas or New Year in keeping with Carinthian tradition. She continued to do this until the outbreak of World War II after which her daughter, Rosita Salaba, renewed it in 1954 with the aid of the Ranger, Mr Bob McCracken. The formation of the Weindorfer Memorial Committee in the 1960s has since continued the tradition each New Years Day in appreciation to Weindorfer for his part in establishing the National Park and arousing the interest of so many people in the conservation of Cradle Valley before and after his death.

This symbol of remembrance inadvertently became the third factor in why Kate has been forgotten and there are two reasons why. One is that it is an Austrian custom and Kate was an Australian citizen and the other is that Kate and Gustav are not buried in the same location. His grave is at the mountain with no indication on his tombstone that he was married and Kate's grave is at the Don, miles away. Therefore each year when the annual memorial service is held commemorating Weindorfer's contribution to Tasmanian history and conservation, his role is reinforced and Kate's role becomes more and more remote.

Plate 46: Kate, aged about 26.
Photo: Courtesy R. Hadrill.

Circumstances from 1914 until 1920 were such that this oversight is understandable and until now Kate has never been examined in isolation to Weindorfer. I acknowledge the fact that she has been mentioned in various books and articles pertaining to him but information about her has often been derived from secondary sources which have not always been

51

accurate. As stated in the Introduction the purpose of this book has not been to undermine the Weindorfer legend but to extend it by revealing the woman who stood resolutely behind him and supported him in every way she could. It is fitting that Kate, Weindorfer's wife and best friend, be acknowledged and remembered for her role in establishing Tasmania's beautiful Cradle Mountain-Lake St. Clair National Park.

APPENDIX ONE

Family Details 1

Thomas Pressland Cowle I

b. unknown in Devon, England
d. 1877 in Hobart, Tasmania
m.
  Mary Wigg
  b. 9.11.18?, in Norfolk,
    England
  d. 1877

1. **Anne Caroline**
   b. 9.5.1831
   d.
   n.m.

2. **Emily**
   b. 1832
   d. 1836
   n.m.

3. **Thomas Pressland**
   b. 27.2.1833
   d. 11.5.1894
   m. 13.5.1855
     Emma Cleaver

4. **Charles Tobin**
   b. 15.5.1835
   d.
   m.
     Marguerite Lewers

5. **Mary-Anne Wilson**
   b. 27.1.1838
   d.
   m. 13.10.1855
     Alfred Wilkins

6. **James**
   b. 25.7.1839
   d. c. 1884
   m. 5.9.1867
     Mary Frances Nicholas

7. **William**
   b. 4.6.1841
   d. Dec. 1841
   (aged 6 months)

APPENDIX TWO

Family Details 2

Thomas Pressland Cowle II

b. 27.2.1833, London
d. 11.5.1894, Devonport
m. 13.5.1855
1. **Emma Cleaver**
   b. 27.2.1833
   d. 27.10.1890
   m.1855
2. **Emily Mary Johnson
   (nee Littlewood)**
   b. .. 1833
   d. 23.4. 1913
   m. 1894 (no issue)

1. **Thomas Pressland (Press)**
   b. 22.10.1858
   d. 25.8.1907
   m.
   **Evelyn Emma unknown surname
   (Eva)**
   b.
   d. .. 11.1936
   1. Violet Evelyn
   2. Dorothy Laura Pressland

2. **Frederick William (Freddy)**
   b. 8.9.1860
   d. 28.11.1889

3. **Emma Caroline Mary (Carrie)**
   b. 20.4.18..
   d.
   n.m.

4. **Kate Julia**
   b. 19.7.1863
   d. 29.4.1916
   m. 1.2.1906
   Gustav Weindorfer
   b. 23.2.1874, Austria
   d. 5.5.1932

5. **Blanche Eleanor**
   b. 30.11.1865
   d. 18.9.1948
   m. 25.8.1897
   Stephen Priest
   b. 25.5.1873, Canada
   d. 5.6.1939
   1. Laura Blanche
   2. Kathleen Eleanor (Katie, Kit)
   3. Pressland (Press)
   4. Charles

APPENDIX TWO

Family Details 2 (continued)

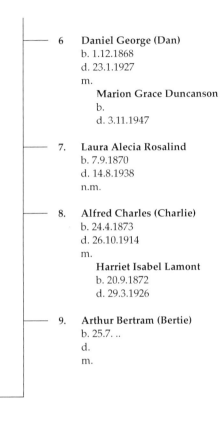

6   Daniel George (Dan)
     b. 1.12.1868
     d. 23.1.1927
     m.
         Marion Grace Duncanson
         b.
         d. 3.11.1947

7.   Laura Alecia Rosalind
     b. 7.9.1870
     d. 14.8.1938
     n.m.

8.   Alfred Charles (Charlie)
     b. 24.4.1873
     d. 26.10.1914
     m.
         Harriet Isabel Lamont
         b. 20.9.1872
         d. 29.3.1926

9.   Arthur Bertram (Bertie)
     b. 25.7. ...
     d.
     m.

BIBLIOGRAPHY

Primary Documents:

Cowle Family papers, held by Mr. Robin Hadrill, Launceston.

Cowle Family papers, held by Mr. Evelyn Graves, Deloraine.

Supreme Court of Tasmania, Probate Department, Wills and Affidavits of assets and Liabilities for: Thomas Pressland Cowle II; Thomas Pressland Cowle III; Kate Julia Weindorfer; Daniel George Cowle and Emily Mary Cowle.

Tasmanian State Archives, Smith Family File, File nos.: NS234/16/7; NS234/19/16; NS234/27/1; NS234/12/2; NS234/12/3.

Trebilco Family documents, held by Mrs AS Trebilco, Devonport.

Victorian Field Naturalists Club, Minute Book, 1901-1907.

Victorian Field Naturalists Club, Membership Lists 1904, 1905 & 1906.

Secondary Documents:

Cowle, K.J., 'Notes of a Visit to Mount Roland', in Victorian Field Naturalists Club, Victorian Naturalist, vol. 20, 1903.

Cowle, K.J., 'Excursion to Yan Yean', in Victorian Field Naturalists Club, Victorian Naturalist, vol. 20, 1903.

Kershaw, J.A., 'Excursion to Yarra Glen' in Victorian Naturalist, vol. 21, May 5 1904.

Register of Births, Death & Marriages, Fingal District, Record of Birth of Kate Julia Cowle, 1863.

Register of Births, Death & Marriages, Launceston District, Record of Marriage of T.P. Cowle II and Emma Cleaver, 1855.

Register of Births, Death & Marriages, Leven District, Record of Death of Kate Julia Weindorfer, 1916.

Parks & Wildlife Service, maps of Cradle Mountain area showing sites of land held by Weindorfer.

Parks & Wildlife Service, floor plans of Waldheim Chalet.

State Forestry Commission, Map of Haslemere Parish at St. Marys, undated.

The North-Western Advocate, and Emu Bay Times, 19.2.06, 17.2.06 & 6.3.06.

The North-West Post, October 28, 1890.

The North-West Post, May 12, 1894.

Weindorfer, G. 'Two Botanists in the Cradle Mountains, Tasmania, in Victorian Naturalist, vol. 28, April 1912.

Interviews - personal and by telephone:

Mr. Hugh Hadrill, Sandy Bay

Mrs. Phyllis Martin, Devonport

Mr. Evelyn Graves, Deloraine

Ms. Diana Peltzer

Ms. Ann Stocks

Mrs. Dorothy Filgate

Secondary References:

Bergman, G.F.J., Gustav Weindorfer of Cradle Mountain, Mercury Press Pty. Ltd., Hobart, 1956.

Cyclopædia of Tasmania, vol. 1, part 2, undated.

Devon Historical Society, Devonport 1890, Advocate Printers, Devonport, 1990.

Duff, D., unpublished notes on the Cowle family, 1993.

Pink, K., And Wealth For Toil, Advocate Printers, Burnie, 1990.

Ramsay, C., With The Pioneers, Mercury Press Pty. Ltd., Hobart, 1957.

Reid, O.W., The North East, Ed. Dept. Tas., Hobart, 1977.

Robson, L., A History of Tasmania, Oxford University Press, Melbourne, 1991.

REFERENCES

1. Interview 1.10.93.
2. State Archives File No. NS234/27/1, Weindorfer's Diaries, 1916.
3. Marriage certificate, T.P. Cowle and Emma Cleaver, 13 May 1855.
4. Duff, D., unpublished notes, 1993.
5. Diaries of T.P. Cowle II, Cowle Family papers, held by Mr. E. Graves, Deloraine.
6. See Appendix One.
7. Cowle Family papers, held by R. Hadrill, Launceston.
8. Duff, D., unpublished papers.
9. Cowle family papers held by R. Hadrill.
10. Duff, *op. cit.*
11. Cowle family papers, held by R. Hadrill.
12. Duff *op. cit.*
13. State Archives File No. 78/1122, Cowle Family Papers.
14. Cowle family papers held by R. Hadrill.
15. *loc. cit.*
16. State Archives File No. 78/1222, Cowle Family papers.
17. *The Cyclopedia of Tasmania, vol.1, part II.*
18. Duff, *op. cit.*
19. Cowle family papers held by R. Hadrill.
20. *loc. cit.*
21. Duff, *op. cit.*
22. *loc. cit.*
23. Cowle family papers held by R. Hadrill, letter dated 9 January 1880.
24. *loc. cit.*
25. *loc. cit.*
26. *loc. cit.*
27. *loc. cit.*
28. Marriage certificate, *op. cit.*
29. Information supplied by R. Cowle, Fingal Historical Society.
30. Cowle family papers, held by E. Graves, Deloraine.
31. See Appendix 2.
32. *loc. cit.*
33. Cowle Family papers, held by R. Hadrill
34. T. P. Cowle's Diaries, 1870-79, held by E. Graves, Deloraine.
35. *loc. cit.*
36. *loc. cit.*

37. Diaries of T.P. Cowle II, *op. cit.*
38. *loc. cit.*
39. See Appendix 2.
40. Diaries of T.P. Cowle II, *op. cit.*
41. *loc. cit.*
42. *loc. cit.*
43. Cowle Family papers, held by R. Graves.
44. *loc. cit.*
45. *loc. cit.*
46. Cowle Family papers, held by R. Hadrill, letter dated 26 August 1879.
47. Cowle Family papers, held by R. Hadrill, letter dated 6 July 1879.
48. Cowle Family papers held by E. Graves.
49. *loc. cit.*
50. *loc. cit.*
51. *loc. cit.*
52. *loc. cit.*
53. *loc. cit.*
54. *loc. cit.*
55. *loc. cit.*
56. *loc. cit.*
57. *loc. cit.*
58. *loc. cit.*
59. *loc. cit.*
60. *loc. cit.*
61. *loc. cit.*
62. *loc. cit.*
63. *loc. cit.*
64. *loc. cit.*
65. *loc. cit.*
66. Cowle Family papers, held by R. Hadrill, letter from Emma to Blanche.
67. letter dated 8 May 1879, *op. cit.*
68. Diary of T.P. Cowle II, *op. cit.*
69. Cowle Family papers, held by E. Graves.
70. Cowle Family papers held by R. Hadrill, letter dated 29 May 1879.
71. Cowle Family papers, held by E. Graves.
72. *loc. cit.*
73. *loc. cit.*

74. Cowle Family papers, held by R. Hadrill, letter dated 18 July 1879.

75. Cowle Family papers, held by R. Hadrill, letter dated 6 July 1879.

76. *loc. cit.*

77. Laura Cowles' personal expense book 1893-1895.

78. Cowle Family papers, held by R. Hadrill, letter dated 18 August 1879.

79. Cowle Family papers, held by R. Hadrill, letter dated 18 July 1879.

80. George, M., letter dated 2 November 1993: This comet was in an almost parabolic orbit around the Sun, and at this time was well placed for southern observers. The comet's closest approach to the Sun in 1880 was at approximately 1 pm, January 28, passing 800,000 kms. from the centre of the Sun, placing it less than 150,000 kms. from the Sun's surface, which is very close considering the Sun's diameter is about 1.4 million kms. It would have been seen at its best at the time of Fred Cowle's letter to his sister Blanche.

81. Cowle Family papers, held by R. Hadrill, letter dated 13 February 1880.

82. *loc. cit.*

83. Dan Cowle's diary, 1887.

84. Laura Cowle's personal expenses book, *op. cit.*

85. *loc. cit.*

86. *loc. cit.*

87. Devon Historical Society, Devonport 1890, Advocate Printers, Devonport, 1990, pp. 8 & 15. Dan Cowle's diaries, 1887-1889.

88. Dan Cowle's diary 1887-1889.

89. *loc. cit.*

90. *loc. cit.*

91. *loc. cit.*

92. Cowle family papers held by R. Hadrill, notes written by Laura Hadrill, undated.

93. *loc. cit.*

94. Dan Cowle's diary, 1905.

95. Victorian Field Naturalists Club, membership lists, 1904 & 1905.

96. Bergman, G.F.J., *Gustav Weindorfer of Cradle Mountain*, Mercury Press Pty. Ltd., Hobart, 1959, p.20.

97. Dan Cowle's Diary, 1905.

98. Field Naturalists Club of Victoria, Minute Book, 1901-1907, pp. 87 & 92.

99. *loc. cit.*

100. Telephone conversation with Sheila Houghton, FNCV librarian, 4.11.93.
101. Cowle, K.J. 'Notes of a Visit to Mount Rowland, Tasmania' and 'Excursion to Yan Yean', in *The Victorian Naturalist*, vol. 20, 1903.
102. Field Naturalists Club of Victoria, Minutes of Meeting, 9 November, 1905.
103. *ibid*, 12 December 1904; 16 January 1905; 13 February 1905; 10 April 1905; 11 September 1905.
104. *Victoria Naturalist*, vol. 22, 1905, p. 106.
105. Hardy, A.D., *Victorian Naturalist*, vol. 21, FNCV, May 4 1905, p. 2.
106. Victorian Field Naturalist Club, Minutes of the meeting of the VFNC, 11 April 1904, copied by S. Houghton, 14 March 1993.
107. Bergman, *op. cit.*, p. 14.
108. Cowle, K., *op. cit.*
109. Bergman, *op. cit.*, p. 8.
110. *ibid*, pp. 8-9.
111. *ibid*, p. 9.
112. Bergman, George F.J. 'Gustav Weindorfer - Some Biographical Notes', The Victorian Naturalist, vo. 71, April 1955, p. 193.
113. Dr. C.S. Sutton, 'Gustav Weindorfer', The Victorian Naturalist, vol. XLIX, June 1932, p. 34.
114. Bergman, George F.J., *op. cit.*, p. 193.
115. Bergman, Gustav Weindorfer of Cradle Mountain, p. 10.
116. *ibid*, p. 11.
117. *ibid*, p. 19.
118. *loc. cit.*
119. *ibid*, p. 20.
120. *loc. cit.*
121. *loc. cit.*
122. Dan Cowle's diary, 1905.
123. *loc. cit.*
124. *loc. cit.*
125. Bergman, 'Gustav Weindorfer of Cradle Mountain', *op. cit.*, p. 8.
126. *ibid*, p. 20.
127. Dan Cowle's diary, 1905.
128. Bergman, *op. cit.*, p. 20.
129. Dan Cowle's Diary, 1905.
130. Interview with Mrs. Phyllis Martin, *op. cit.*
131. State Archives File No. NS 234/27/1, Weidorfer's diaries.

132. State Archives File Nos. NS 234/27/1; NS 234/12/2; NS 234/2/ 3, Weindorfer's diaries and Kate's personal letters to him.
133. Cowle family papers, held by Robin Hadrill.
134. Wedding invitation sent to Stephen and Blanche Priest.
135. State Archives File No. NS. 234/27/1, Gustav Weindorfer's diary, 1906.
136. *loc. cit.*
137. Certificate of Marriage between Kate and Gustav.
138. Weindorfer's diary, 1906, *op. cit.*
139. *loc. cit.*
140. *loc. cit.*
141. Bergman, *op. cit.*, p. 22: A collection of mosses and lichen from Mt. Roland were forwarded by Gustav to the Austrian Court Museum for Natural History in Vienna.
142. Telephone discussion with Mr. Ron Bramich of Lower Barrington, son of L.G. Bramich, 24.10.93.
143. Weindorfer's 1906 diary, *op. cit.*
144. *loc. cit.*
145. *loc. cit.*
146. *loc. cit.*
147. The North Western Advocate and Emu Bay Times, letter dated 26 February 1906, edn. 6 March 1906, p. 4.
148. *ibid*, letter dated 17 February, edn. 19 February 1906, p. 4.
149. *ibid*, letter dated 26 February, edn. 6 March 1906, p. 4.
150. *loc. cit.*
151. *loc. cit.*
152. *loc. cit.*
153. *ibid*, letter dated 26 February.
154. Bergman, *op. cit.*, p. 22.
155. Interview with Mrs. Phyllis Martin, 1 October 1993.
156. Bergman, *op. cit.*, p.22.
157. *ibid*, pp. 22-23.
158. *ibid*, p. 23.
159. Interview with Mrs. Phyllis Martin, *op. cit.*
160. Cowle Family papers, held by R. Hadrill.
161. Dan Cowle's Diaries.
162. State Archives File no. NS 234/19/16, letter dated 9 October 1909.
163. *ibid*, letter dated 16 March 1910.
164. State Archives File Nos.: NS 234/27/1; NS 234/12/2; NS 234/12/3, Weindorfer's diaries and Kate's letters.

165. State Archives File No. NS 234/12/2, letters dated 15.3.13; 28.3.13; 7.6.12; 27.10.1913; 20.1.14.
166. Bergman, *op. cit.*, p. 23.
167. *loc. cit.*
168. Trebilco Family papers, held by Mrs. A.S. Trebilco, Devonport.
169. *loc. cit.*
170. *ibid*, p. 25.
171. Weindorfer, G., 'Two Botanists in the Cradle Mountains, Tasmania', in *Victorian Naturalist*, vol. 28, April 1912, pp. 216-223.
172. *loc. cit.*
173. *loc. cit.*
174. *loc. cit.*
175. *loc. cit.*
176. Bergman, *op. cit.*, p. 27.
177. *loc. cit.*
178. *ibid*, p. 28.
179. *loc. cit.*
180. *loc. cit.*
181. State Archives File No. NS 234/19/16, Ronald Smith's Diaries.
182. *ibid*, p. 29.
183. State Archives File no. NS 234/12/2, Lands Dept. receipt no. 96, 16 October 1910.
184. *ibid*, Treasury Revenue Branch Receipt no. 26, 25 April 1911.
185. Bergman, *op. cit.*, p. 29.
186. State Archives File no. NS 234/12/3, letter dated 11 August 1913.
187. Bergman, *op, cit.*, p.30.
188. *ibid*, p. 31.
189. State Archives File no. NS 234/12/3, letter dated 19 November 1913.
190. Bergman, op. cit. p. 30. State Archives File no. NS 234/27/1, Weindorfer's diary, 1913.
191. State Archives File no. NS 234/27/1, Weindorfer's diary, 1913.
192. *loc. cit.*
193. State Archives File no. NS 234/12/3, letter dated 5 August 1913.
194. *ibid*, letter dated 25 August 1913.
195. *ibid*, letter dated 11 August 1913.
196. *ibid*, letters dated 30 April & 15 August 1913.
197. *ibid*, 30 April 1913.
198. *ibid*, letter dated 4 May 1913.

199. *loc. cit.*
200. *ibid*, letter dated 1 August 1913.
201. Weindorfer's diary, 1913.
202. State Archives File no. NS 234/12/3, *op. cit.*, letter dated 28 August 1913.
203. State Archives File no. NS 234/27/1, Weindorfer's diaries.
204. *loc. cit.*
205. State Archives File nos. NS 234/12/2 & NS 234/12/3, assorted letters, descriptions of *Waldheim* and attractions of Cradle Valley written by the Weindorfers.
206. *loc. cit.*
207. *loc. cit.*
208. *loc. cit.*
209. *loc. cit.*
210. State Archives File no. NS 234/12/3, letter dated 11 April 1914.
211. *loc. cit.*
212. State Archives File no. NS 234/27/1, Weindorfer's diary, 1914.
213. *loc. cit.*
214. Bergman, *op. cit.*, p. 37.
215. Weindorfer's diary, 1914.
216. State Archives File no. NS 234/12/3, letter from Kate to Weindorfer's parents, 16 August 1914.
217. Weindorfer's diary, 1914.
218. *loc. cit.*
219. Interview with Mrs. Phyllis Martin, *op. cit.*
220. Weindorfer's 1914 diary.
221. *loc. cit.*
222. Letter dated 16 August 1914, *op. cit.*
223. Weindorfer's 1914 diary.
224. *loc. cit.*
225. *loc. cit.*
226. *loc. cit.*
227. State Archives File no. NS 2324/12/3, letter dated 1 May 1915.
228. *ibid*, letter dated 11 January 1916.
229. *ibid*.
230. *ibid*, 2 letters, one dated 8 November 1915, the other undated.
231. *ibid*, undated letter.
232. *loc. cit.*
233. *loc. cit.*
234. *ibid*, letter dated 27 October 1915.

235. Weindorfer's Diary, 1915, op. cit.
236. Letters file, undated letter
237. *loc. cit.*
238. State Archives File no. NS 234/12/3, letter dated 23 November 1915.
239. *ibid,* undated letter from "The Towers" in Launceston.
240. *ibid,* letters dated 21 December & 28 December 1915.
241. *ibid,* letters dated "Boxing Day", 1915.
242. *ibid,* letters dated 21 December & 28 December 1915.
243. Weindorfer's Diary, 1915.
244. State Archives file no. NS 234/12/3, letter dated 19 January 1916.
245. Weindorfer's diary, 1916.
246. State Archives File no. NS 234/12/3, note from Hitchcock to Weindorfer.
247. Weindorfer's Diary, 1916.
248. *loc. cit.*
249. Births, Deaths & Marriages Register, Central Folio no. C. 0465/1916. *Concise Medical Dictionary,* Oxford University Press, London, 1981, pp. 418-9 & 664.: Nephritis is also known as Bright's Disease and is an inflammatory condition of the kidneys and uraemia a consequence of renal failure caused by waste products accumulating in the blood. It was a common condition caused by infection in the early days. If left untreated it causes death. Modern treatment may include haemodialysis.
250. *loc. cit.*
251. Codicil to Will of Kate Julia Weindorfer, 25 March 1916.
252. Will of Kate Julia Weindorfer.
253. State Archives file no. NS 2324/12/3, letter from the Office of Taxes, Launceston, 14 November 1916.
254. Dan Cowle's diary, 1926.
255. State Archives file no. NS 234/12/3, letter from Bert Cowle to Weindorfer, 19 July 1916.
256. Bergman, *op. cit.,* p. 38.
257. *ibid,* p. 40.
258. *loc. cit.*
259. Interview with Mr. Hugh Hadrill, 10 September 1993.
260. *Victorian Naturalist,* vol. 20, 1903.
261. Weindorfer's diaries, 1914.
262. *ibid,* 1913: He and Kate had just spent 6½ weeks together at the mountain.

263. *ibid*, 1916. State Archives no. NS 234/12/3, letter to Weindorfer 1 May 1916 from Kathie Smith following Kate's death: 'I don't know how to express my heartfelt sympathy to you. It feels as though I'd lost a very dear relation, (and) that is only a thousandth part of your feelings. Please God to help and bless you (and) keep you till he calls you to join your dearest (and) best.'

264. Letter to me from Mrs. Filgate, 17 March 1994.

INDEX